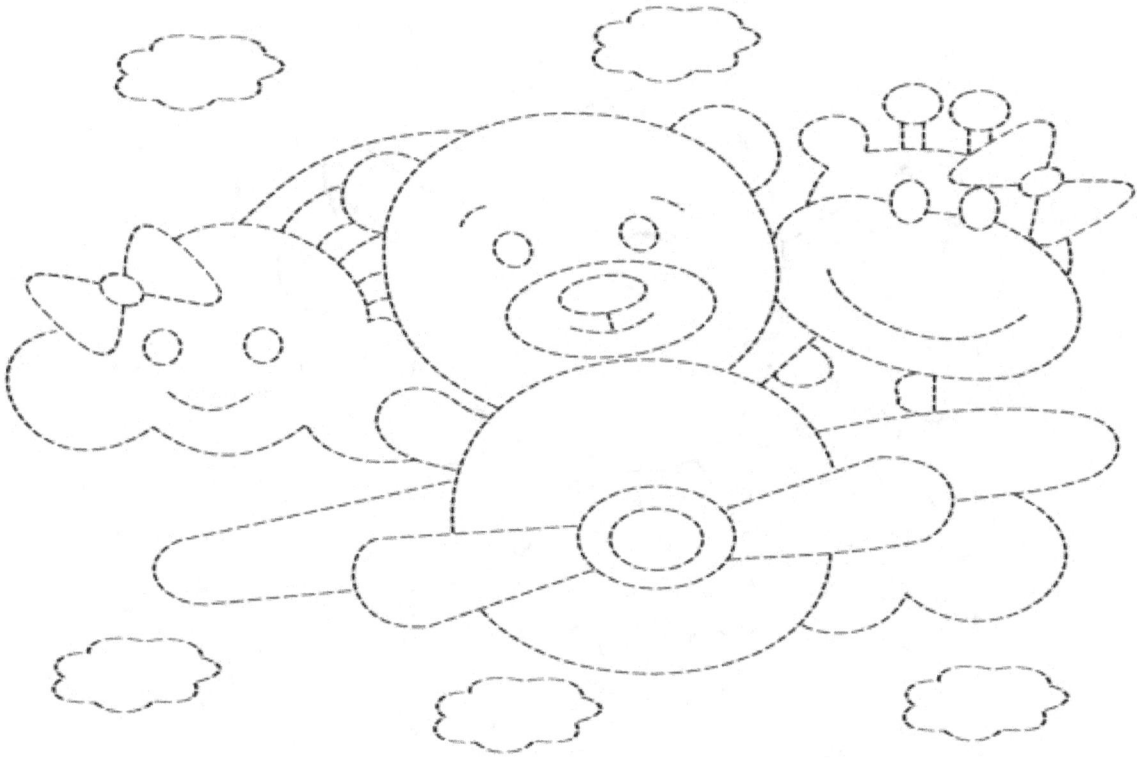

This Colouring Book Belongs To:

_____

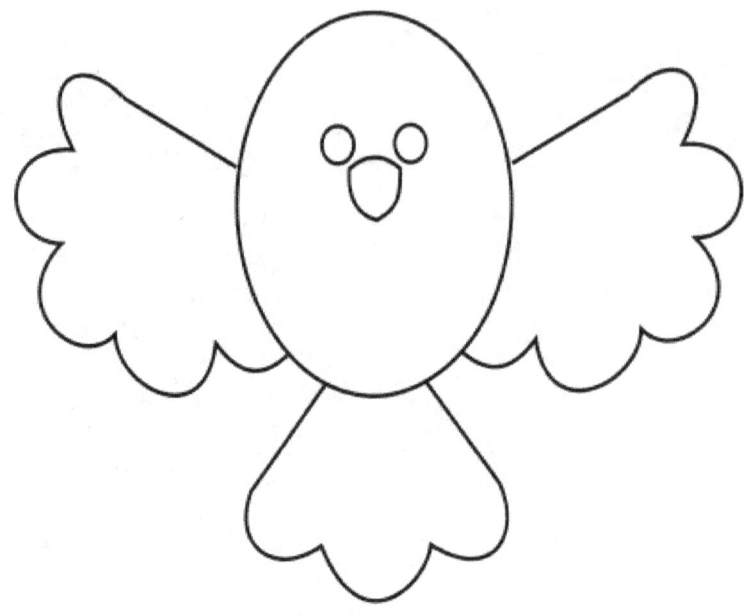

Copyright © 2020 Daniela Paino

Author,Illustration or Publishing Information:

daniela.paino@hotmail.com

Facebook page

Daniela Paino
Author and Illustration of Colouring books.

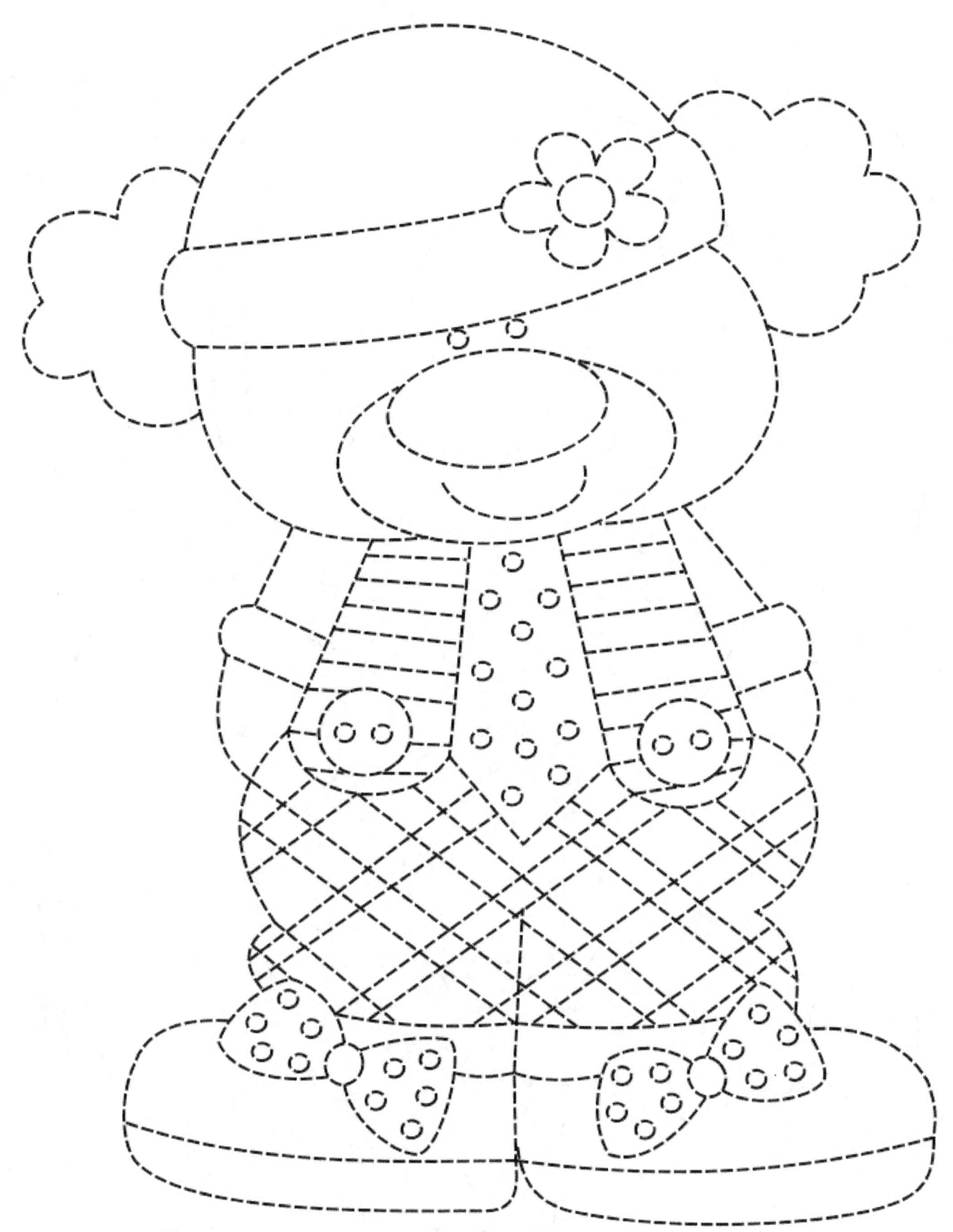

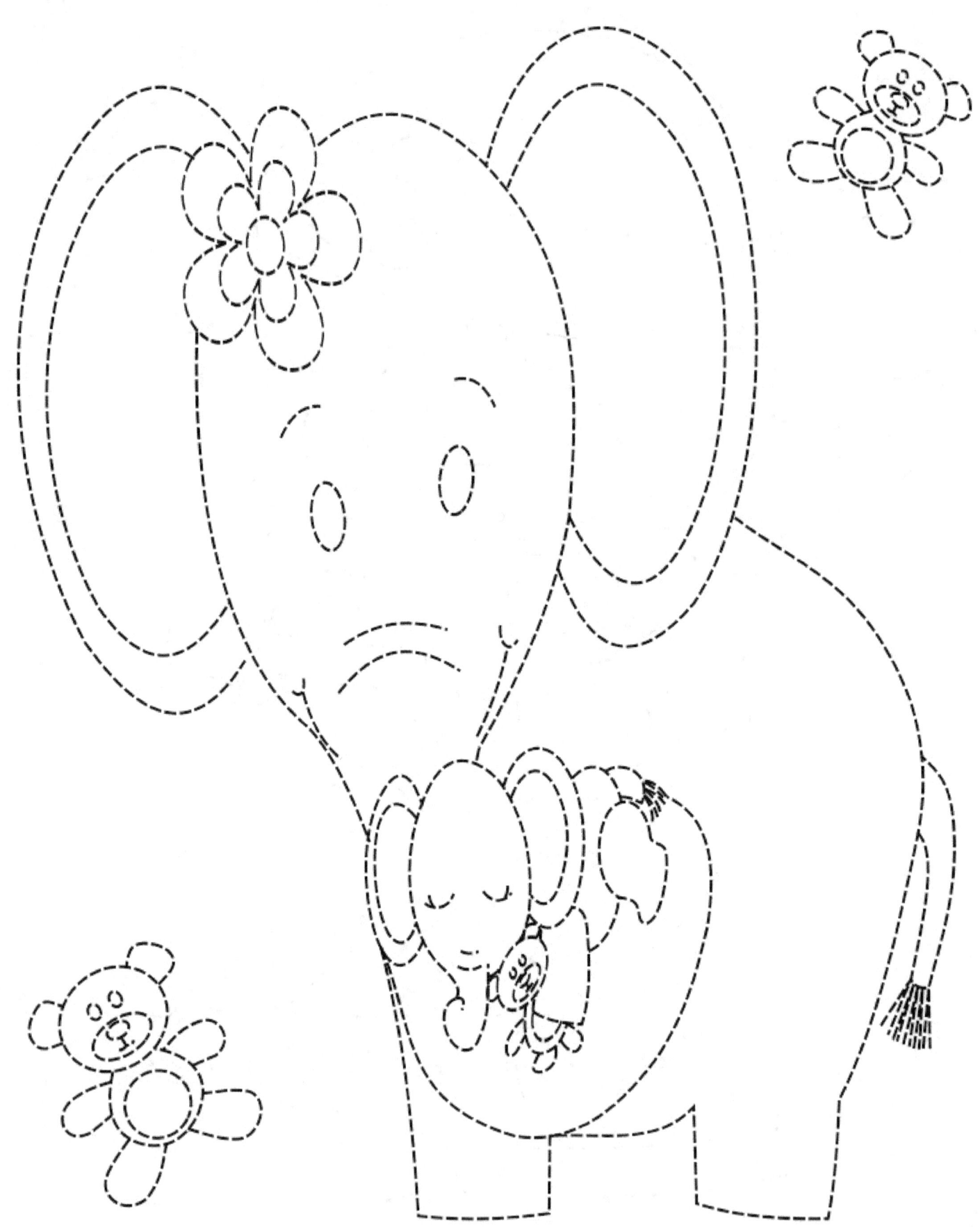

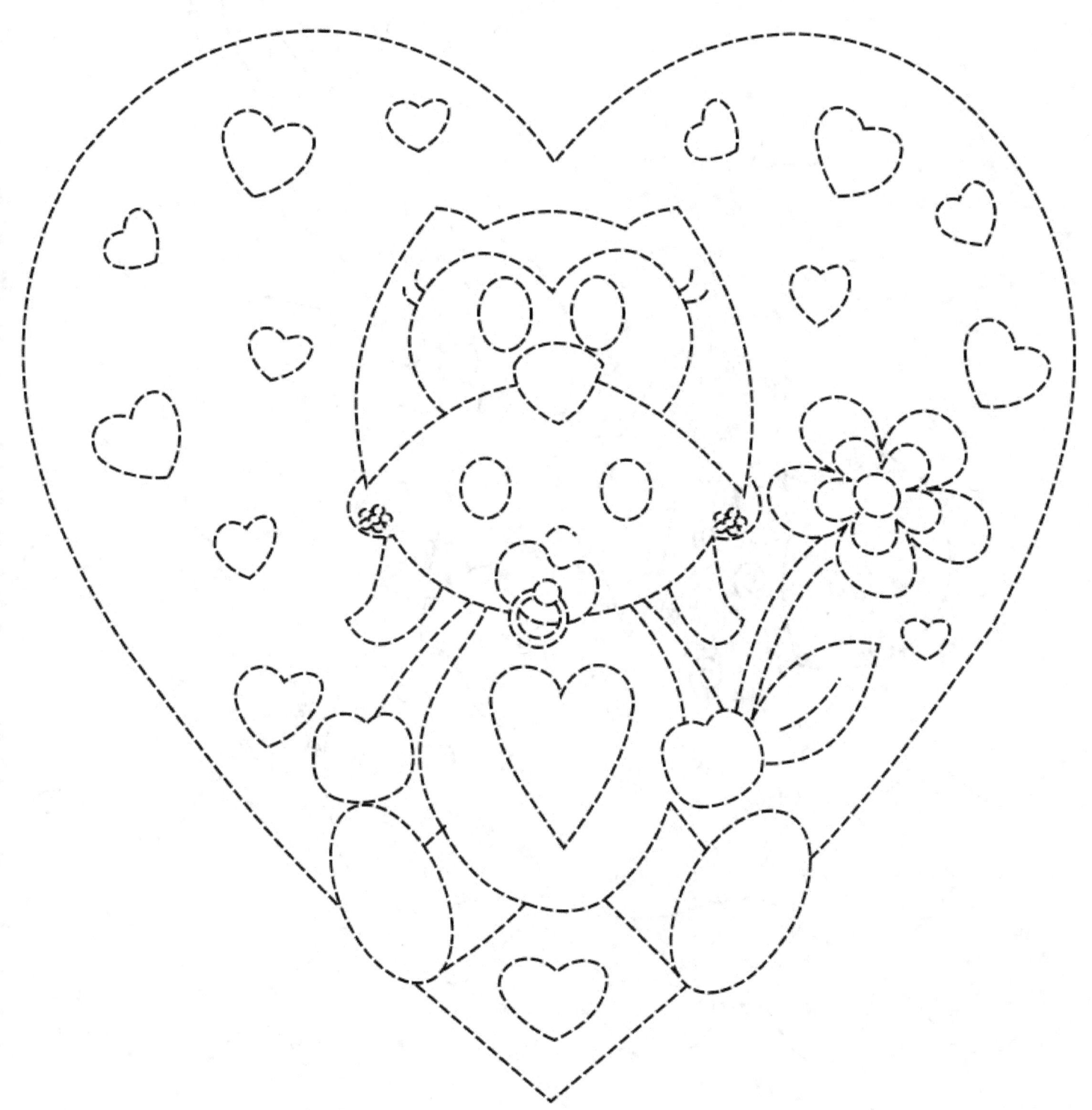

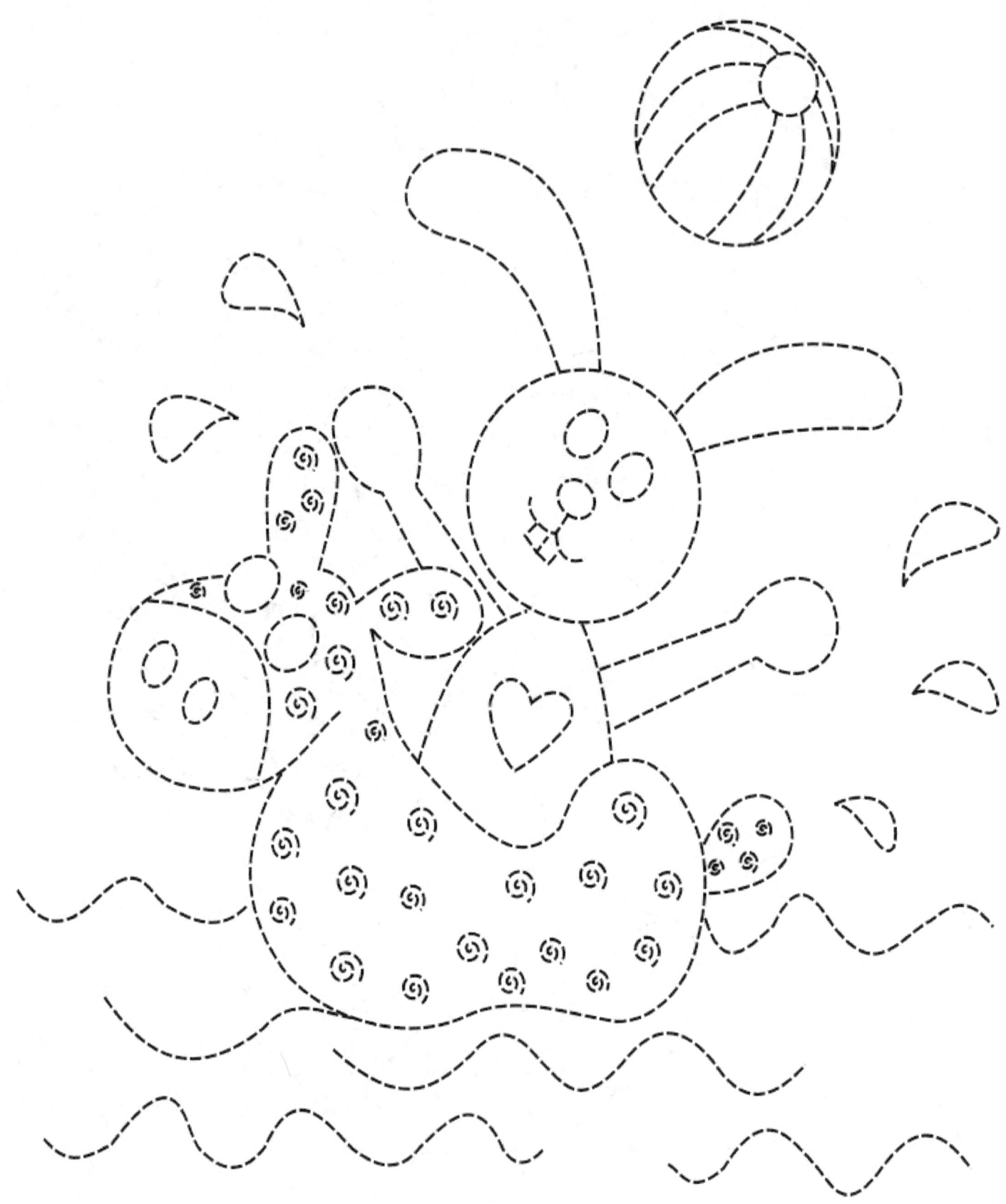

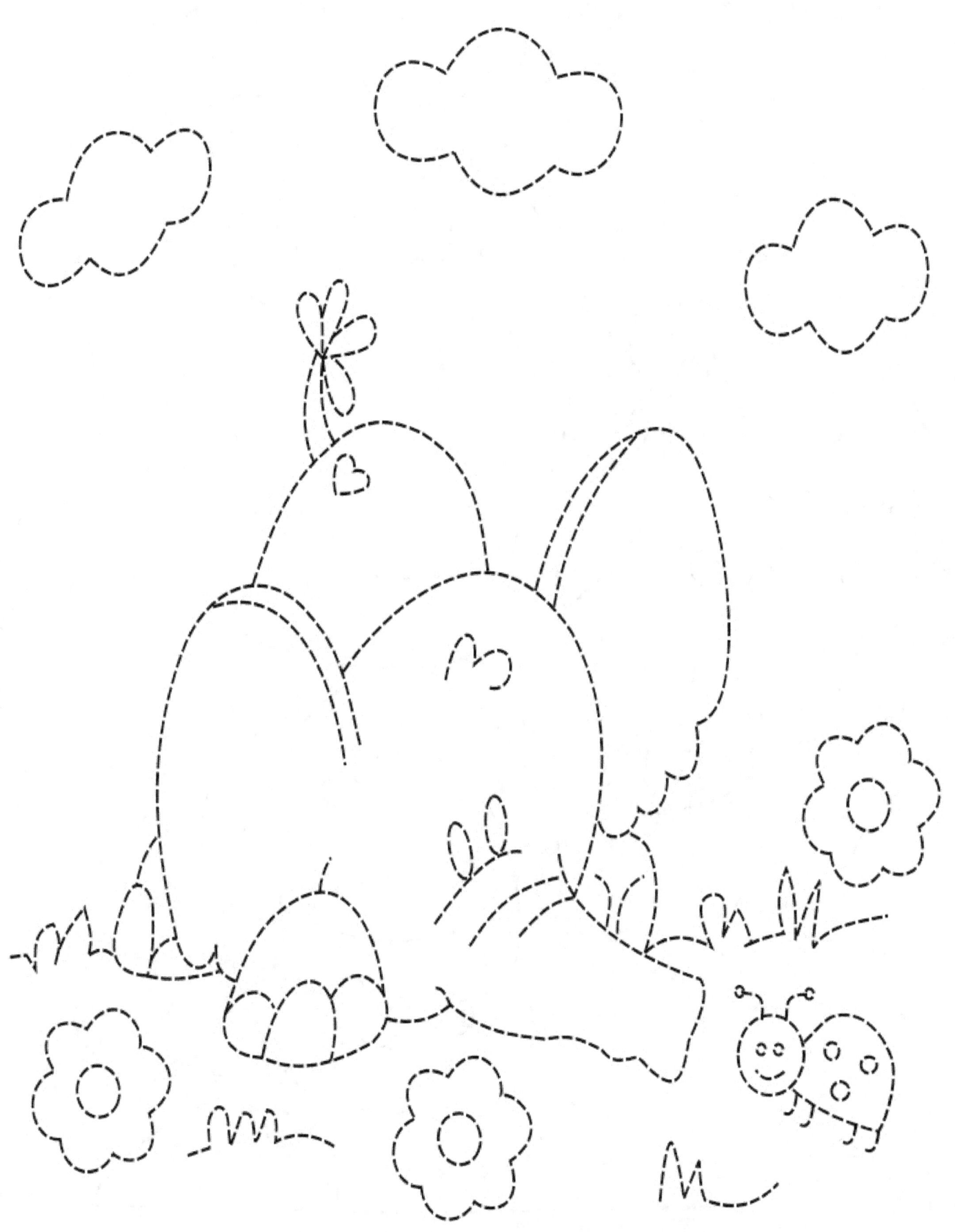

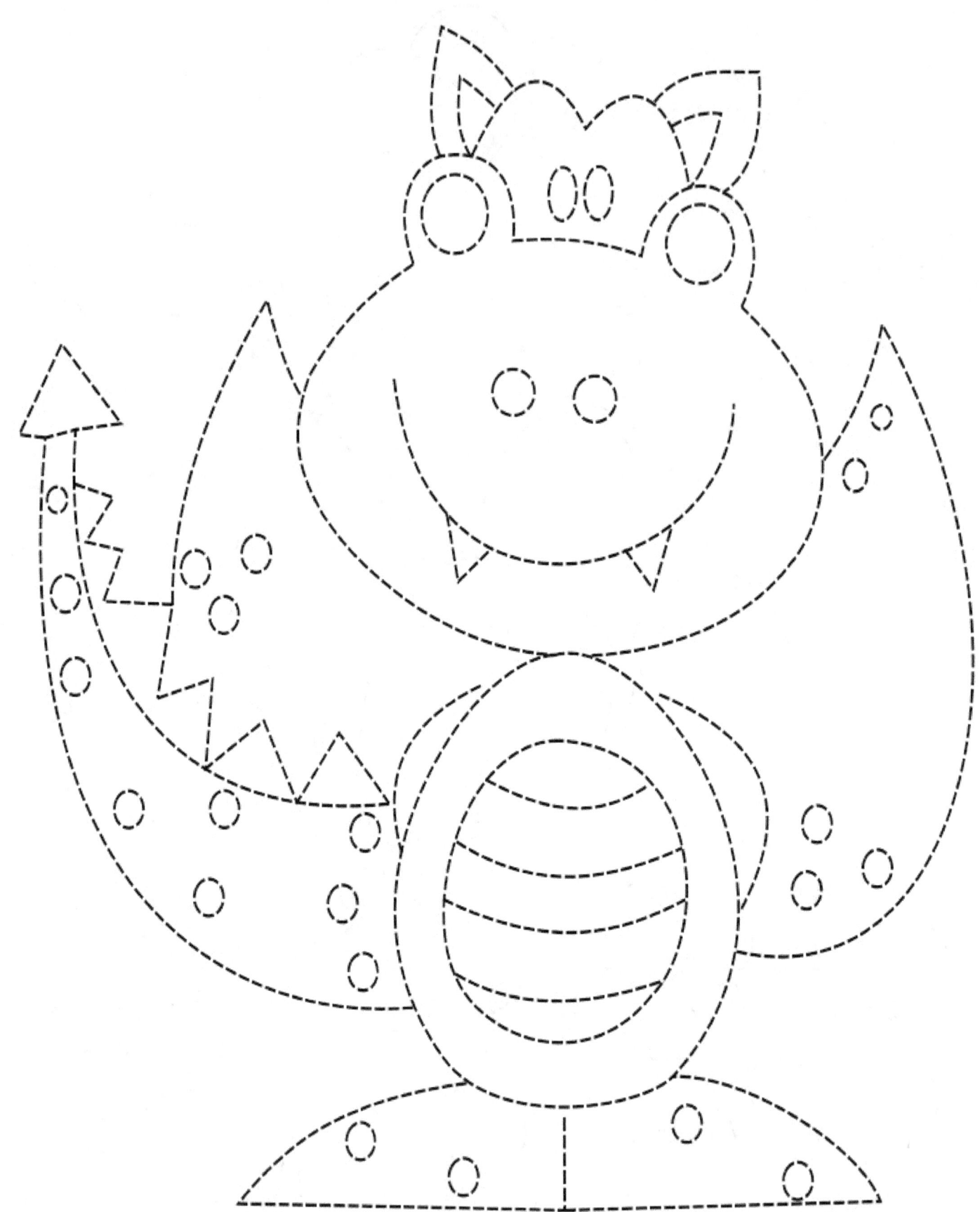

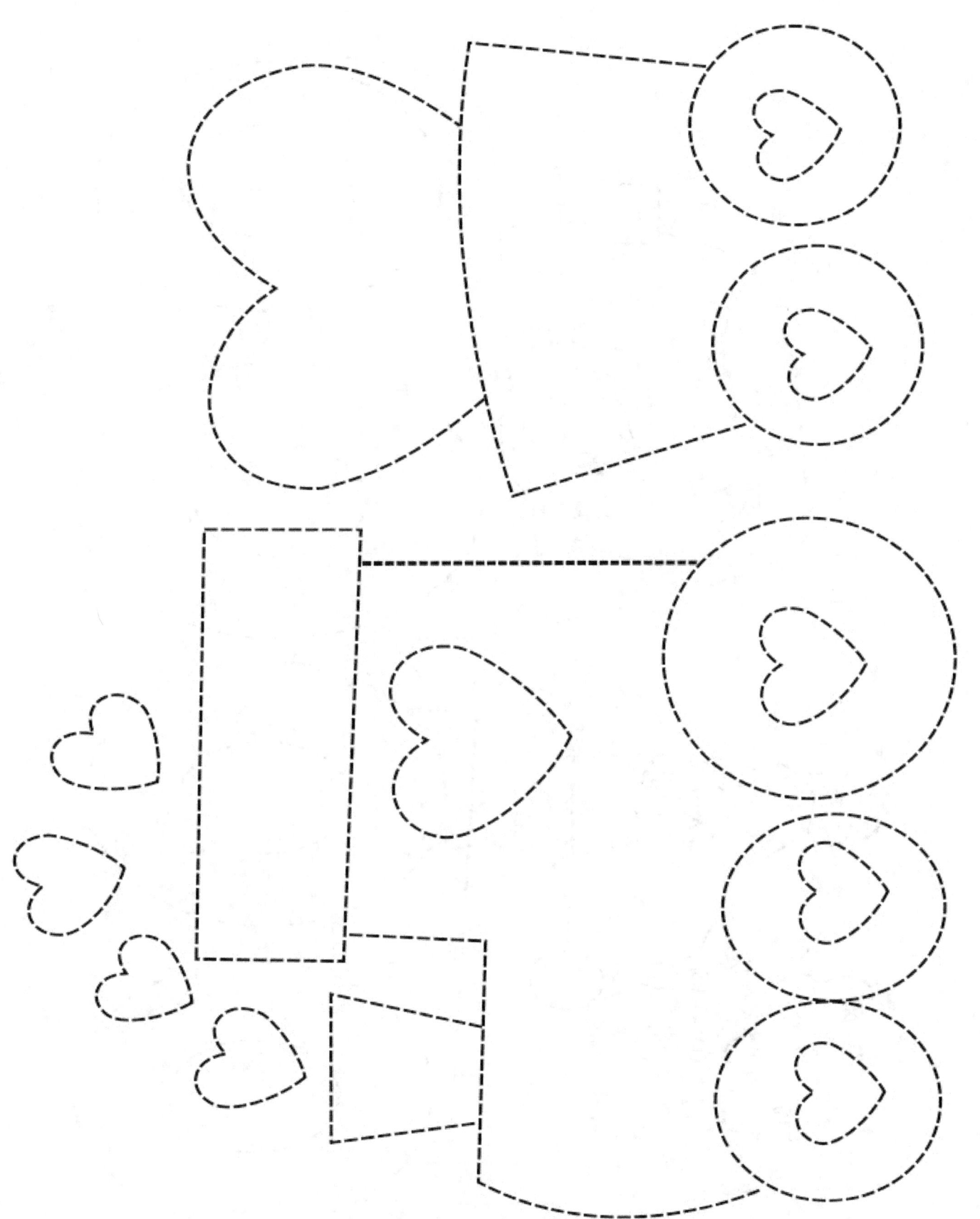

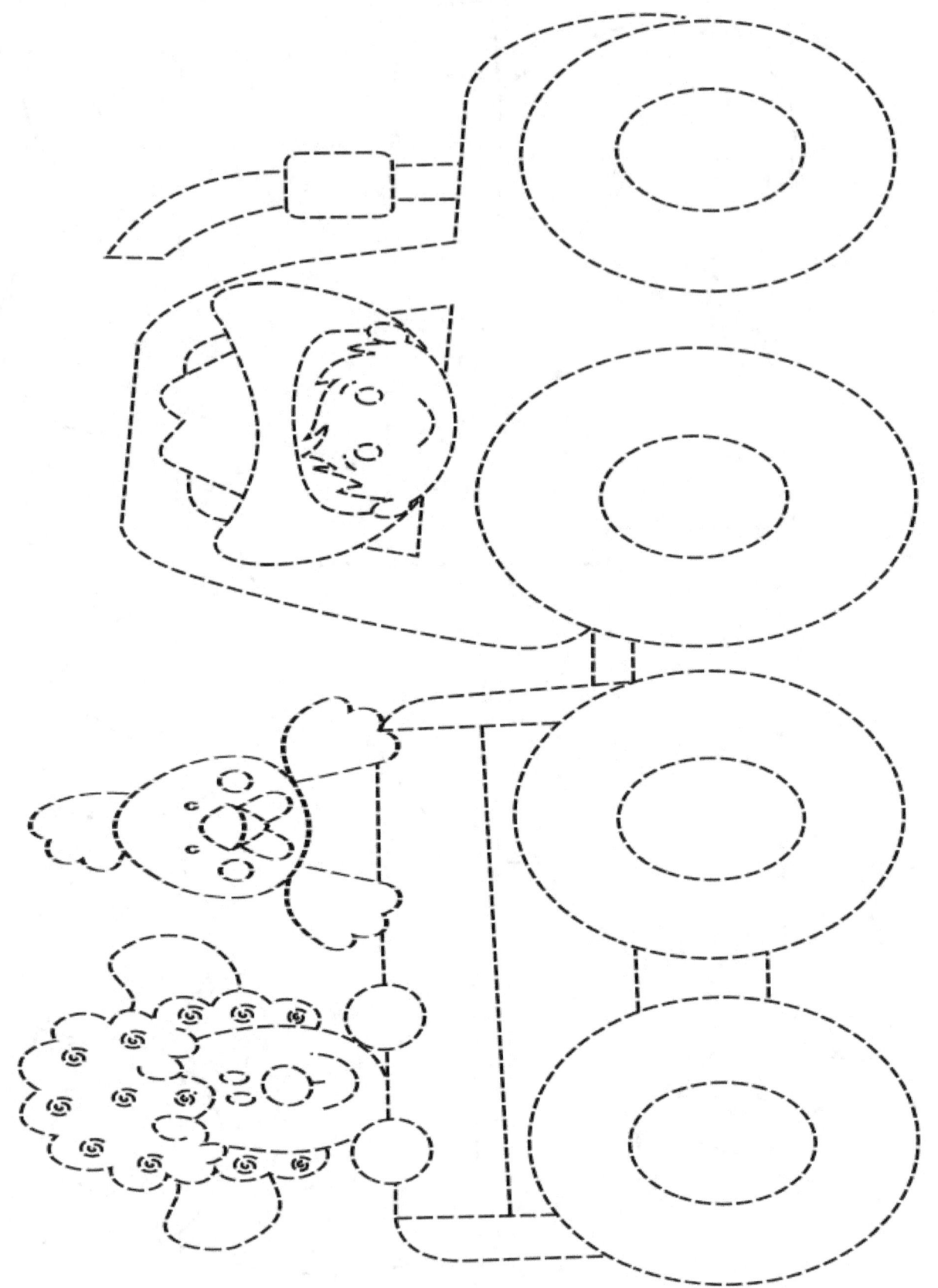

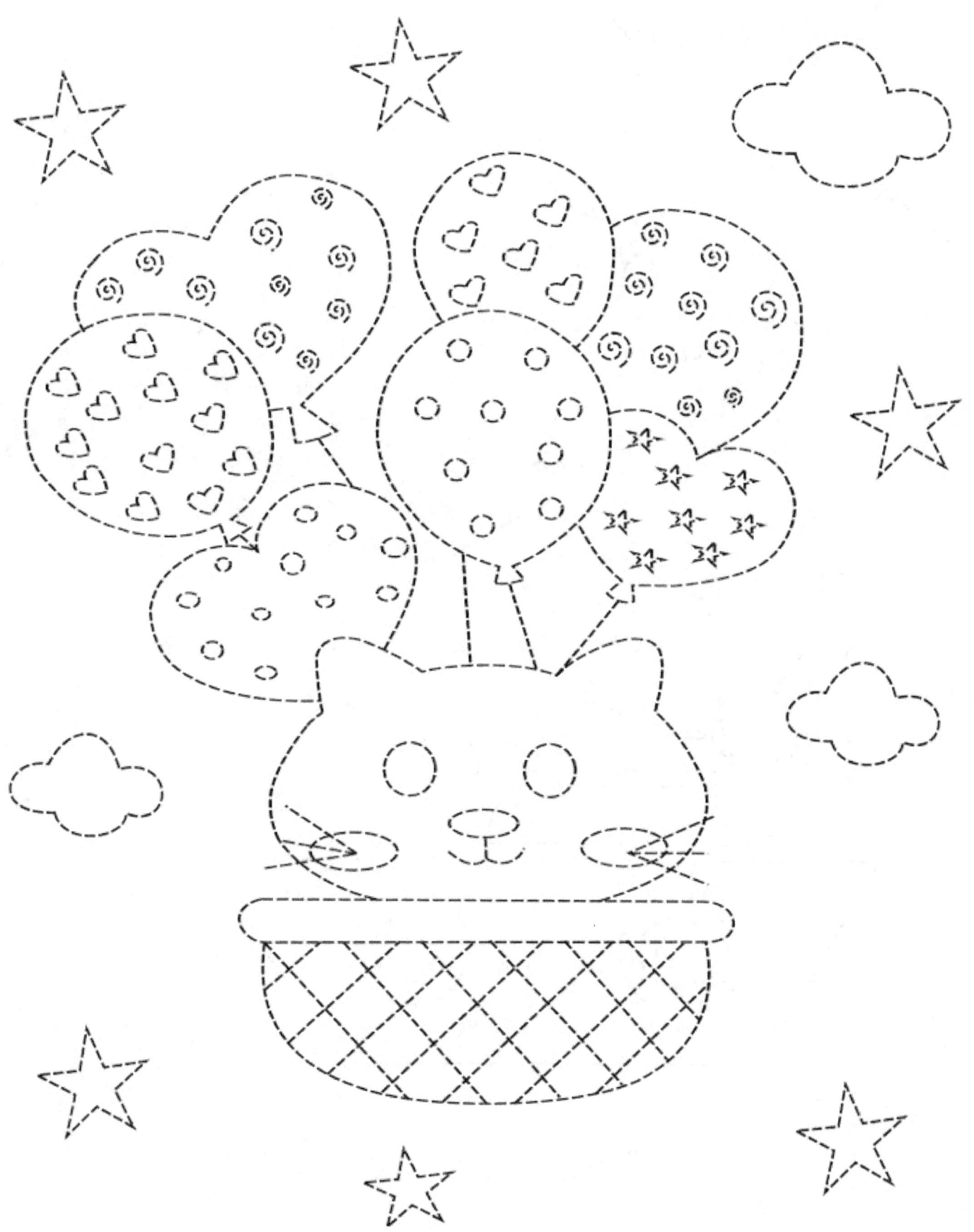

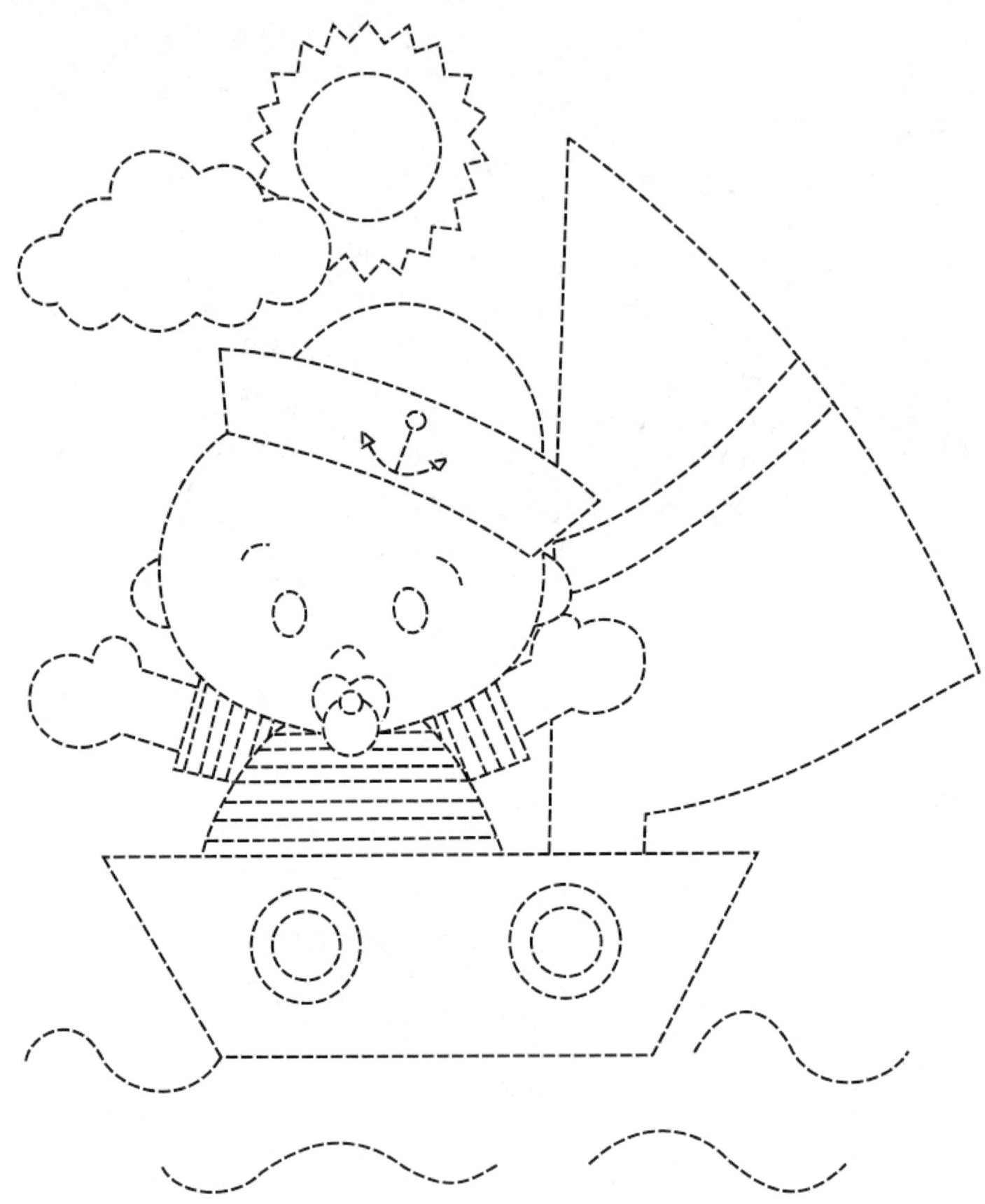

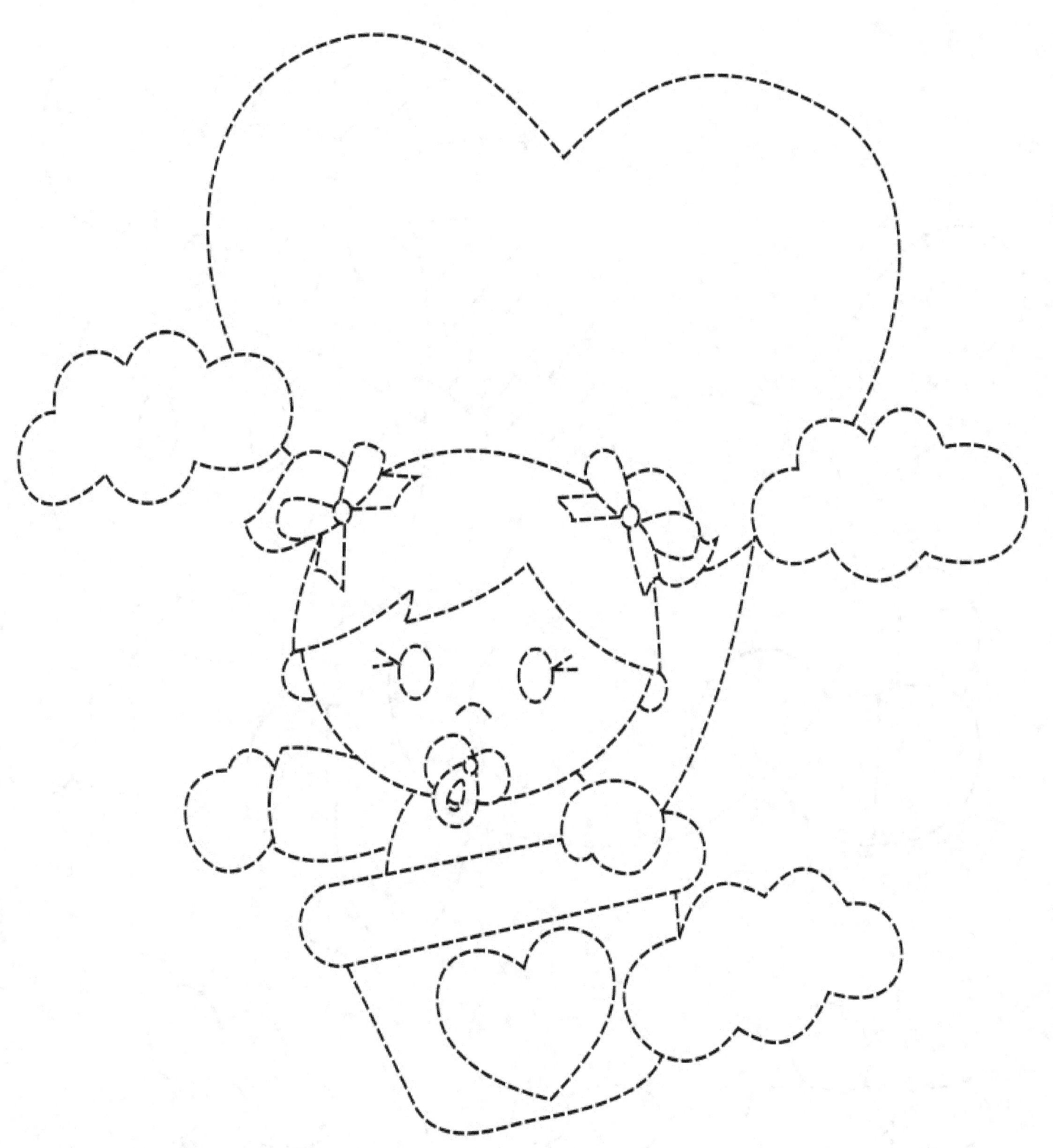

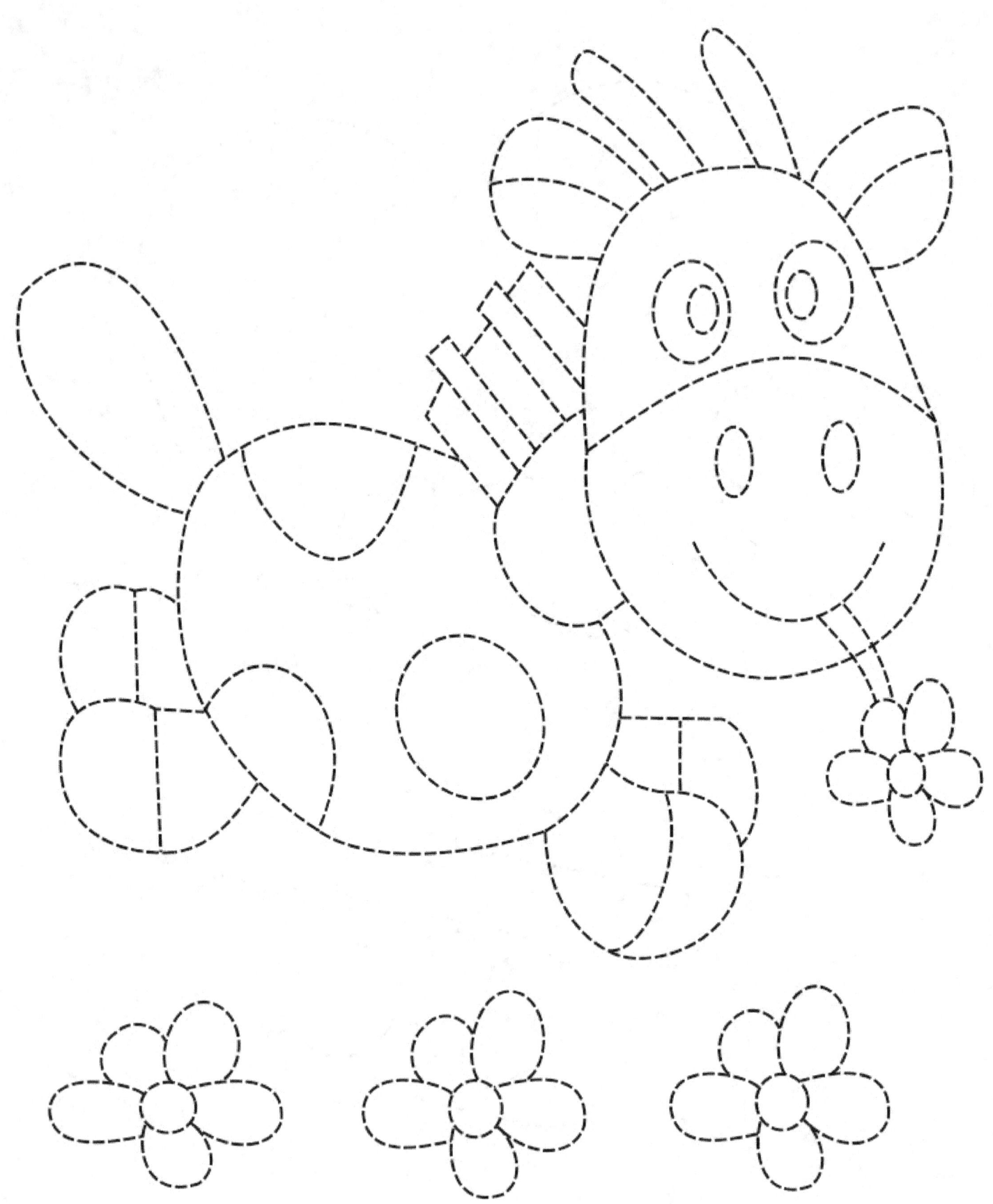

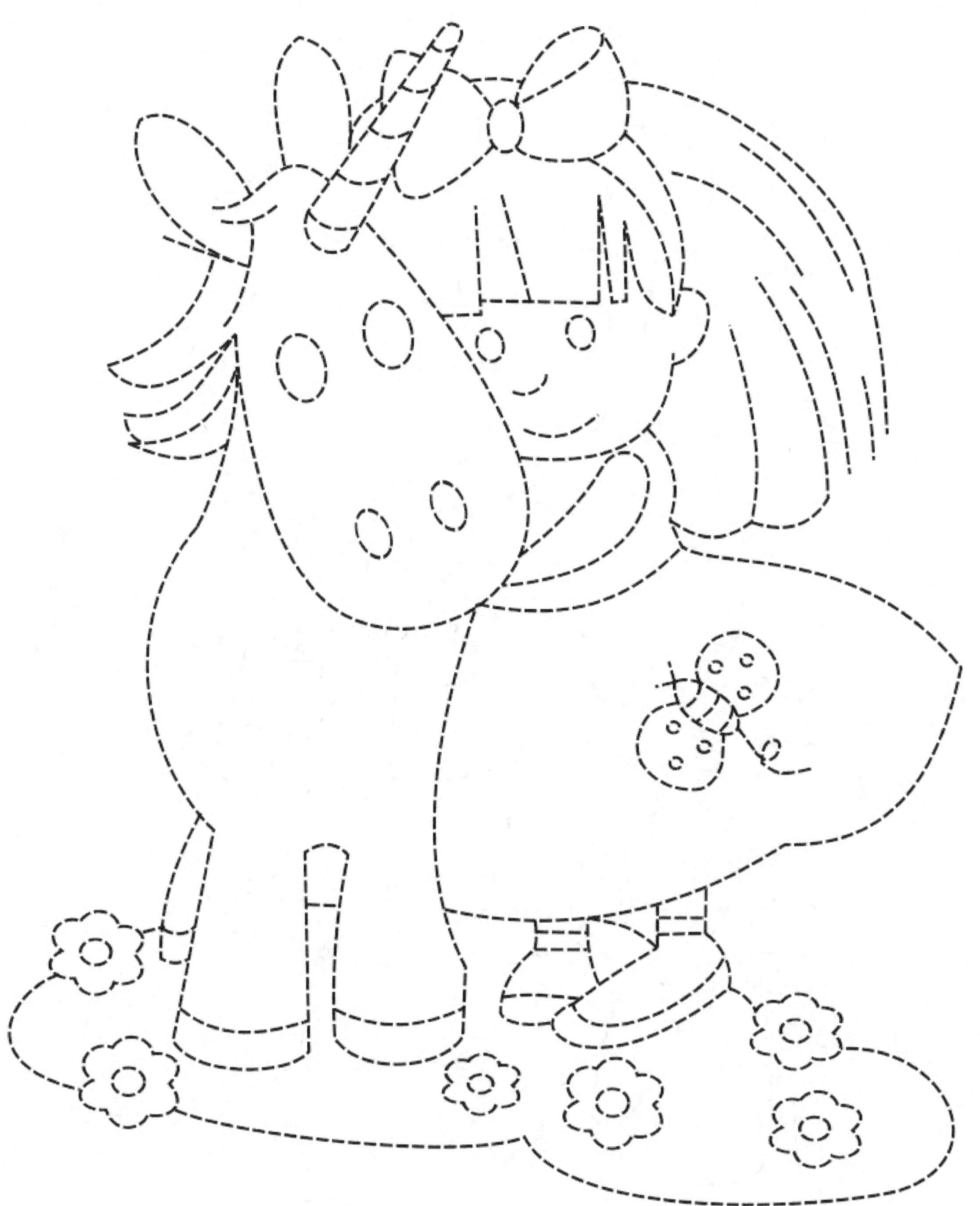

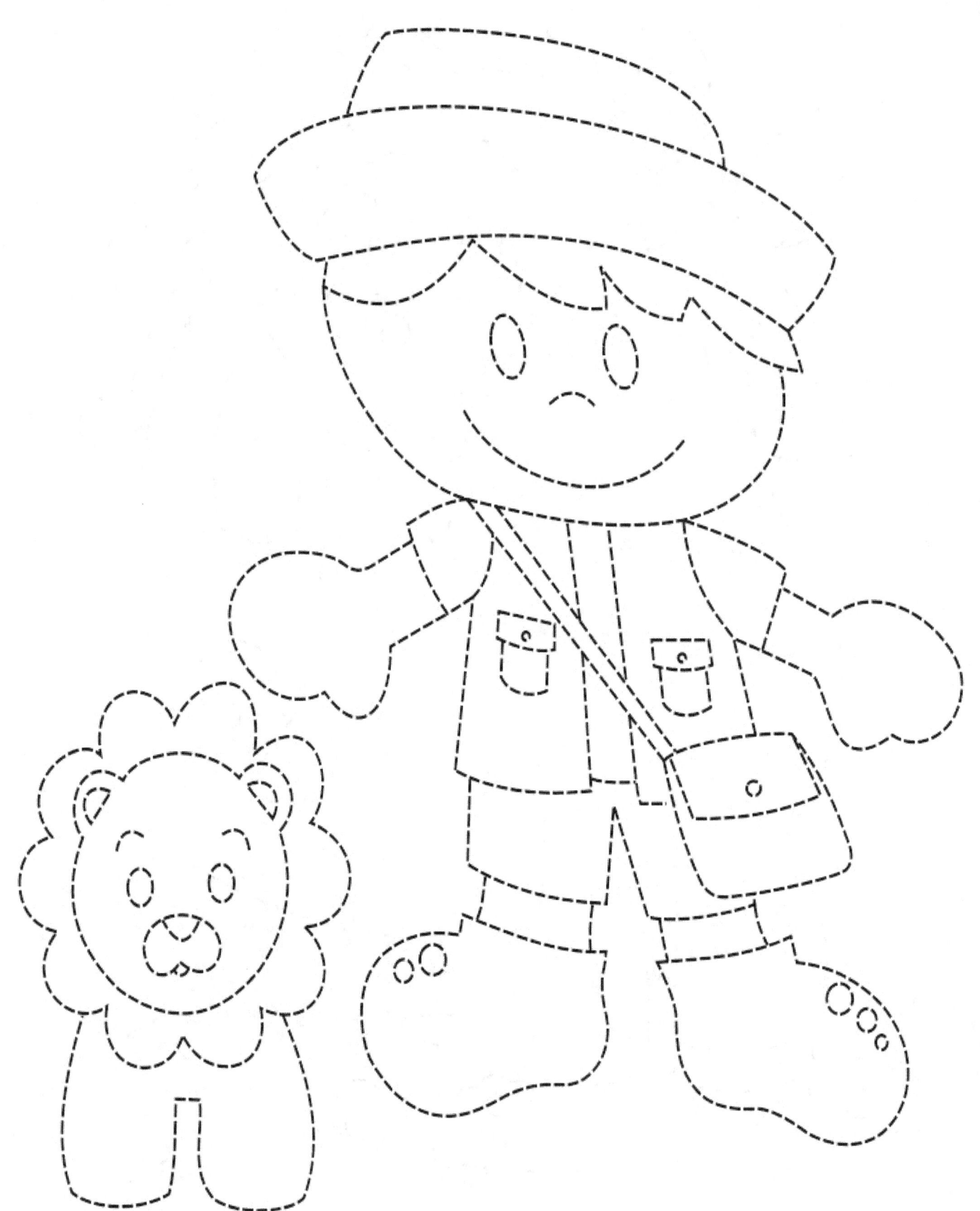

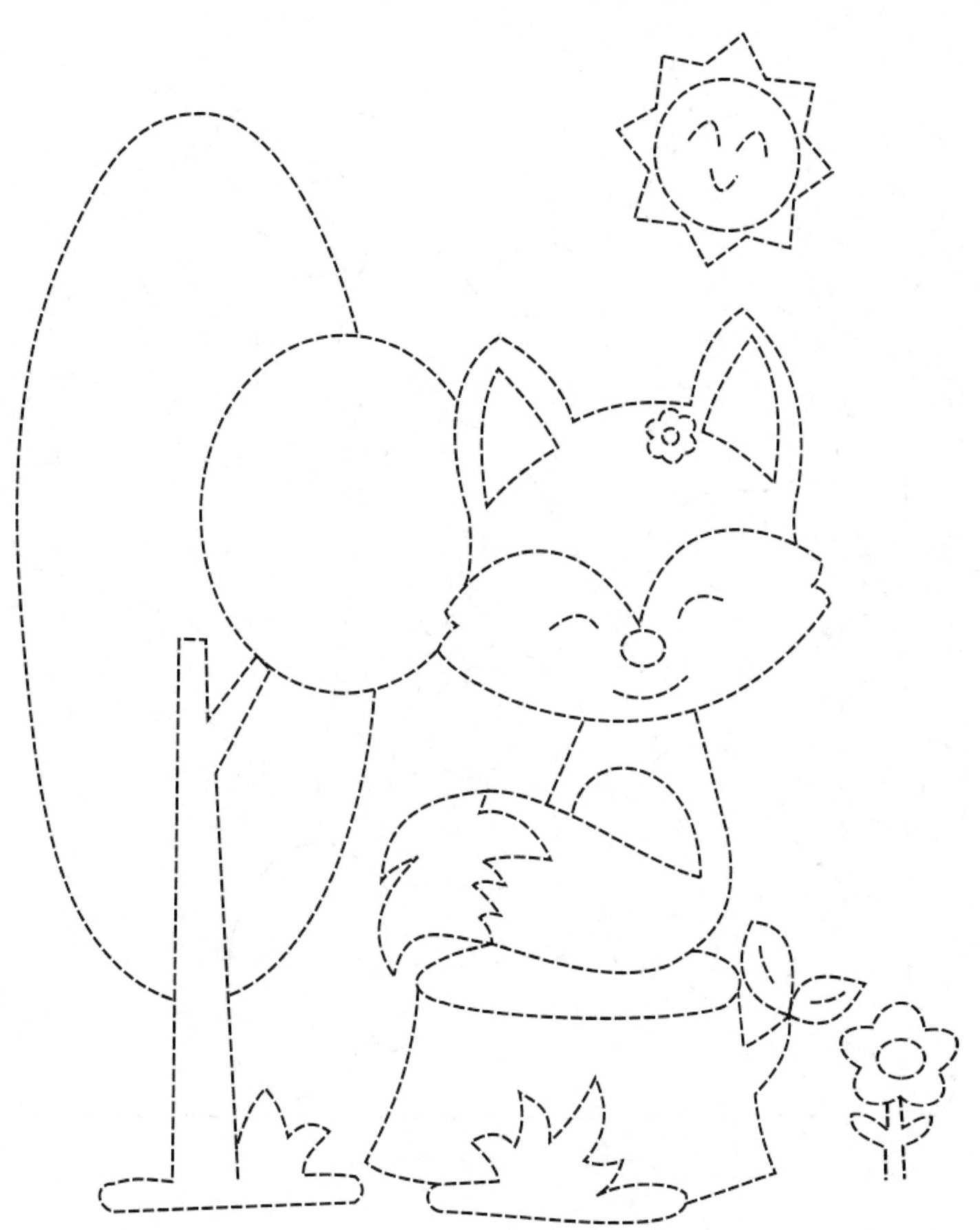

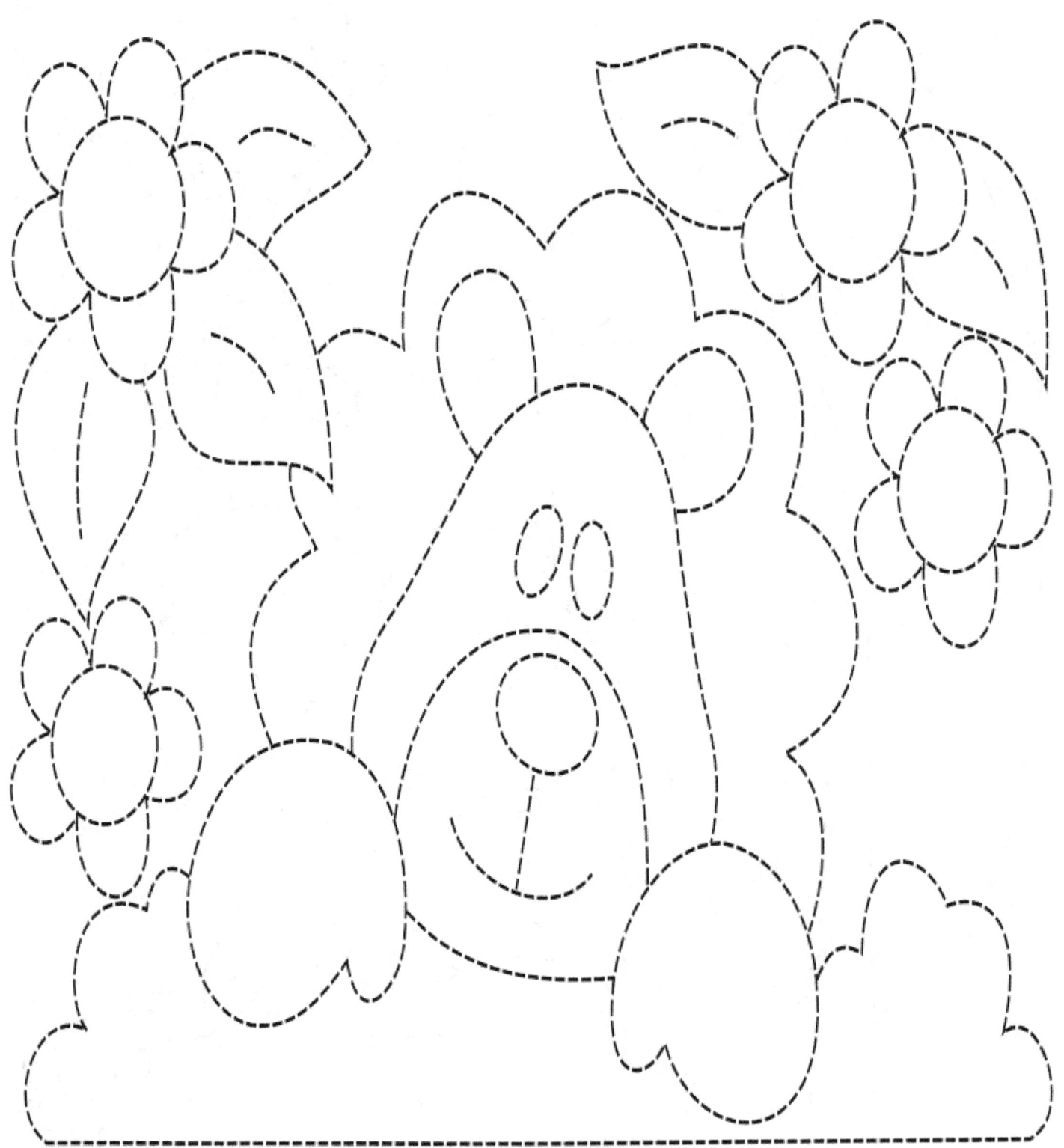

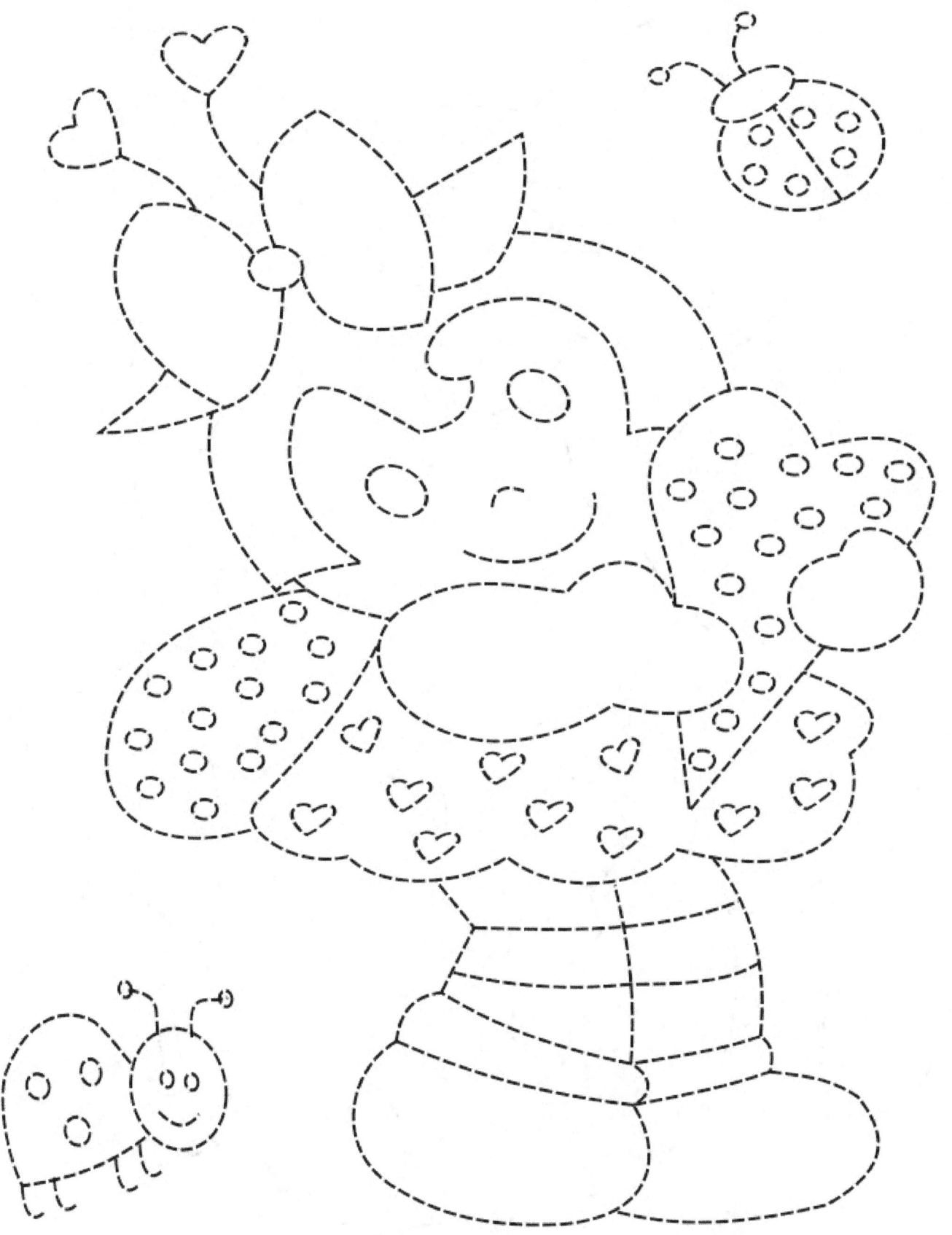

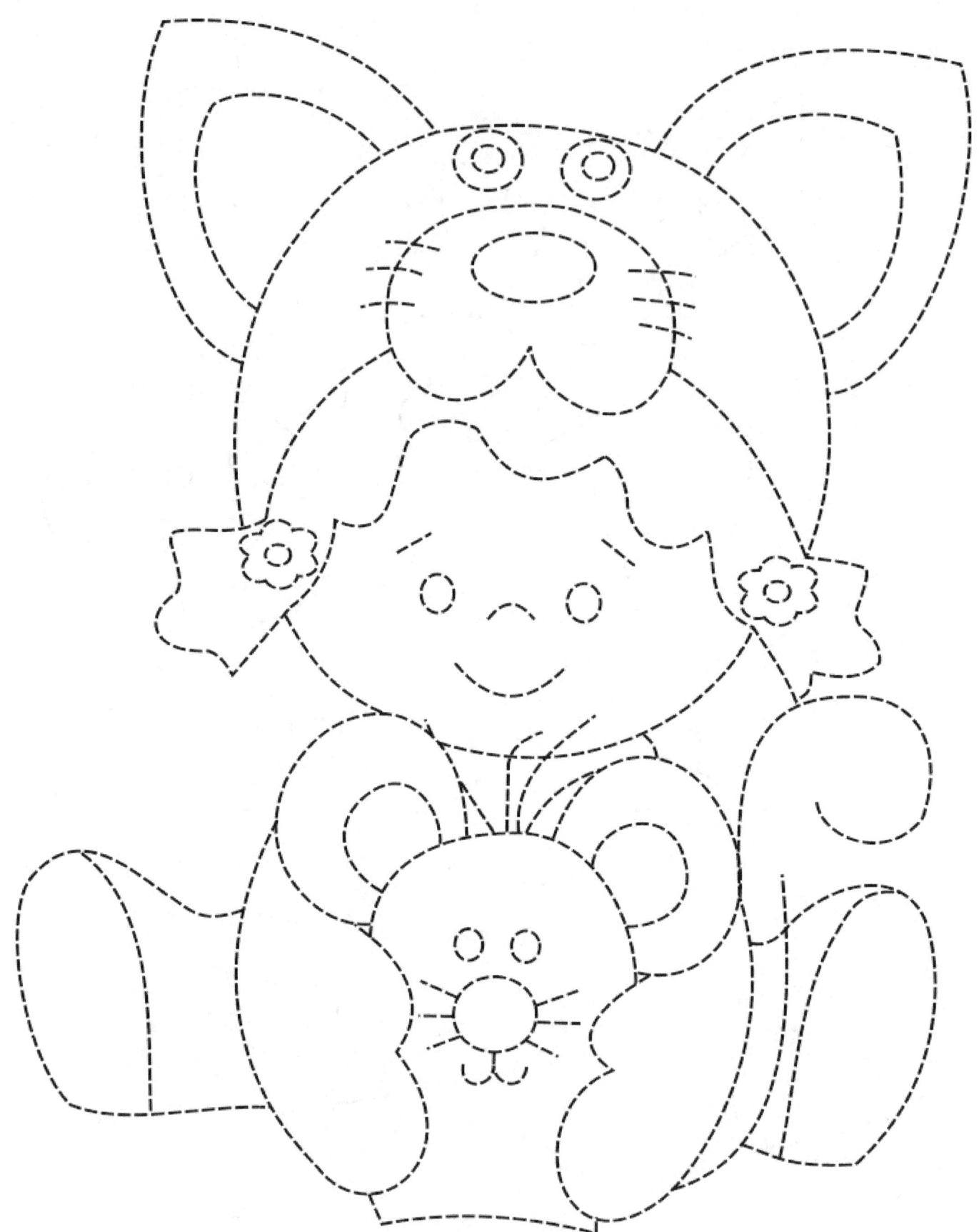

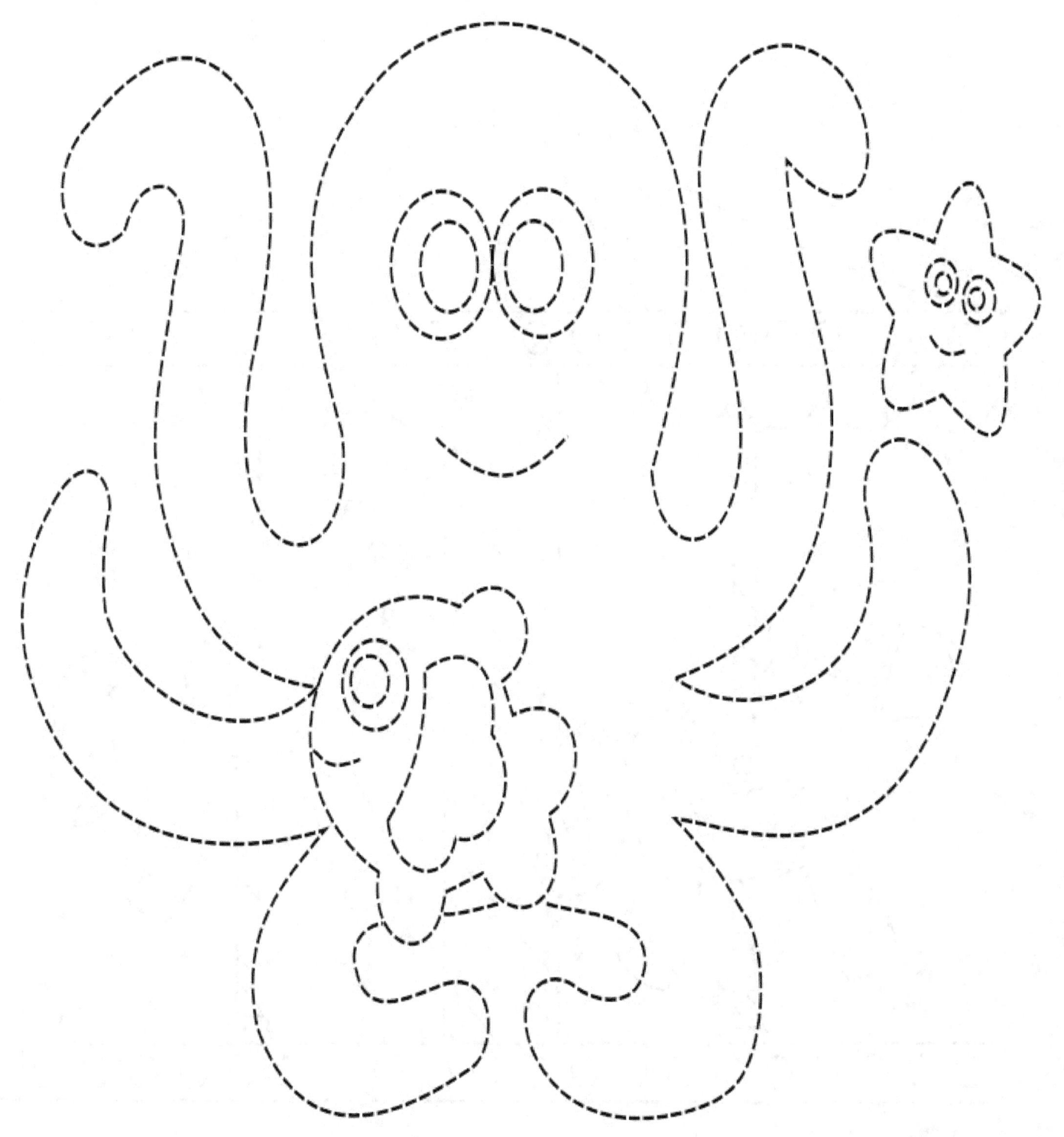

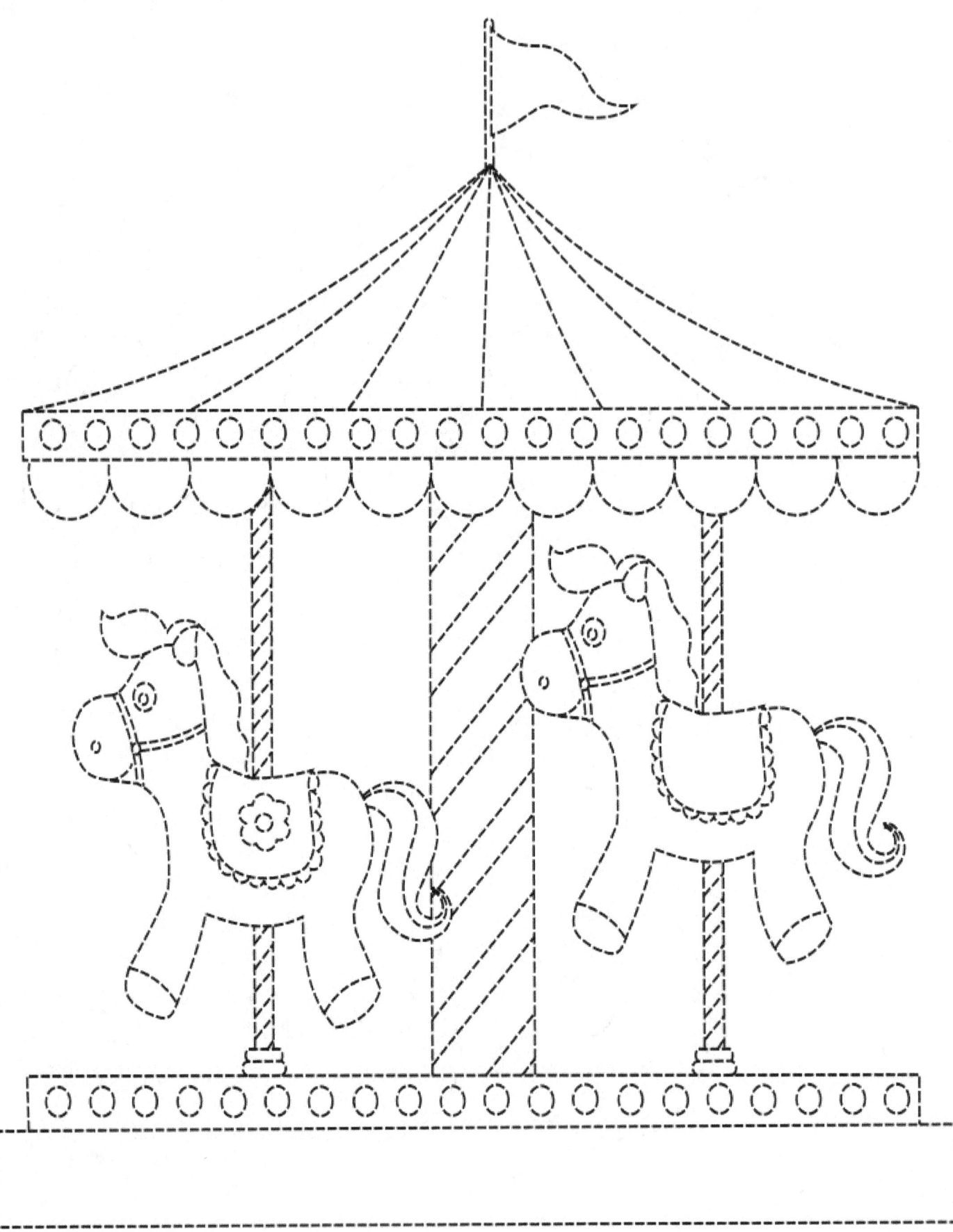

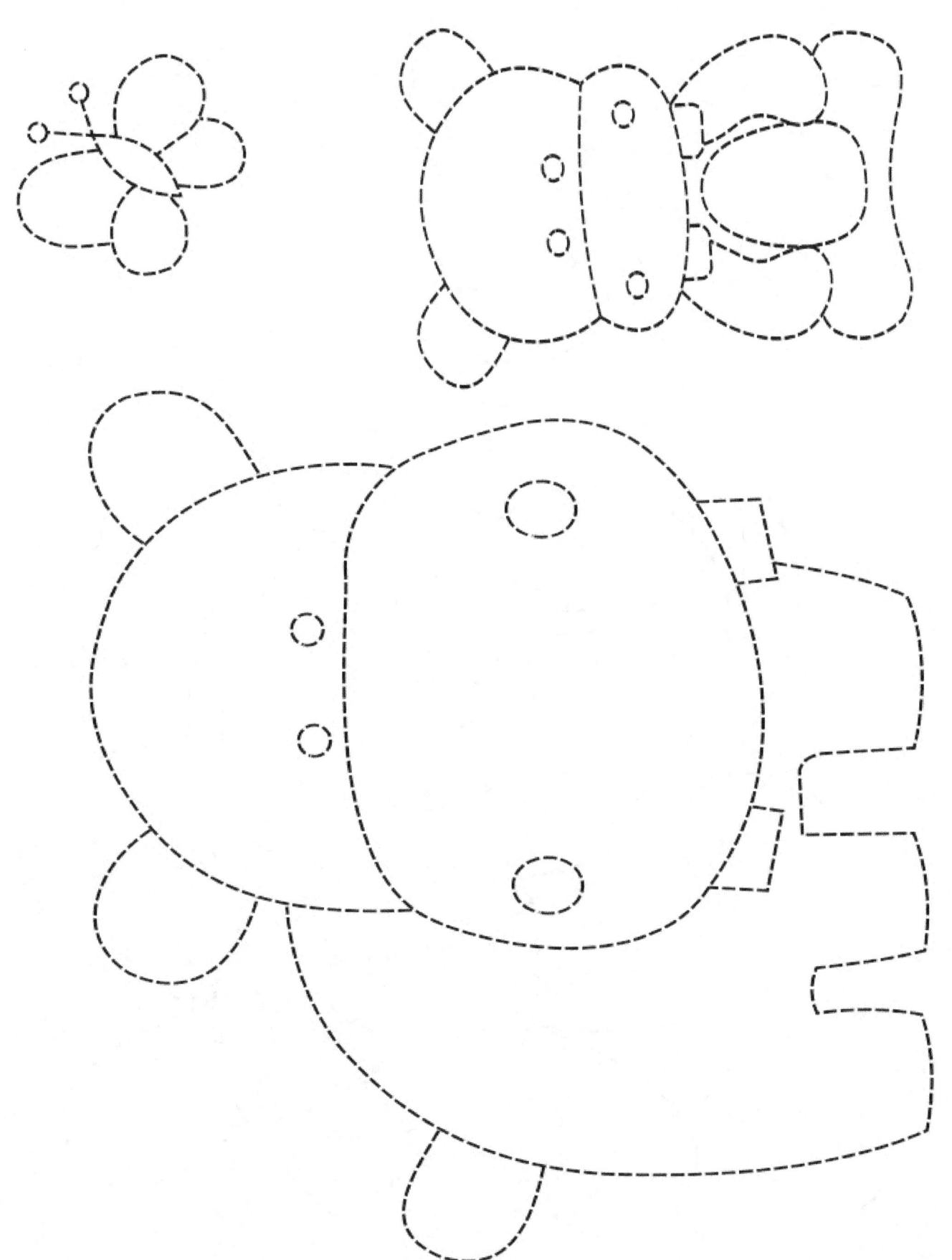

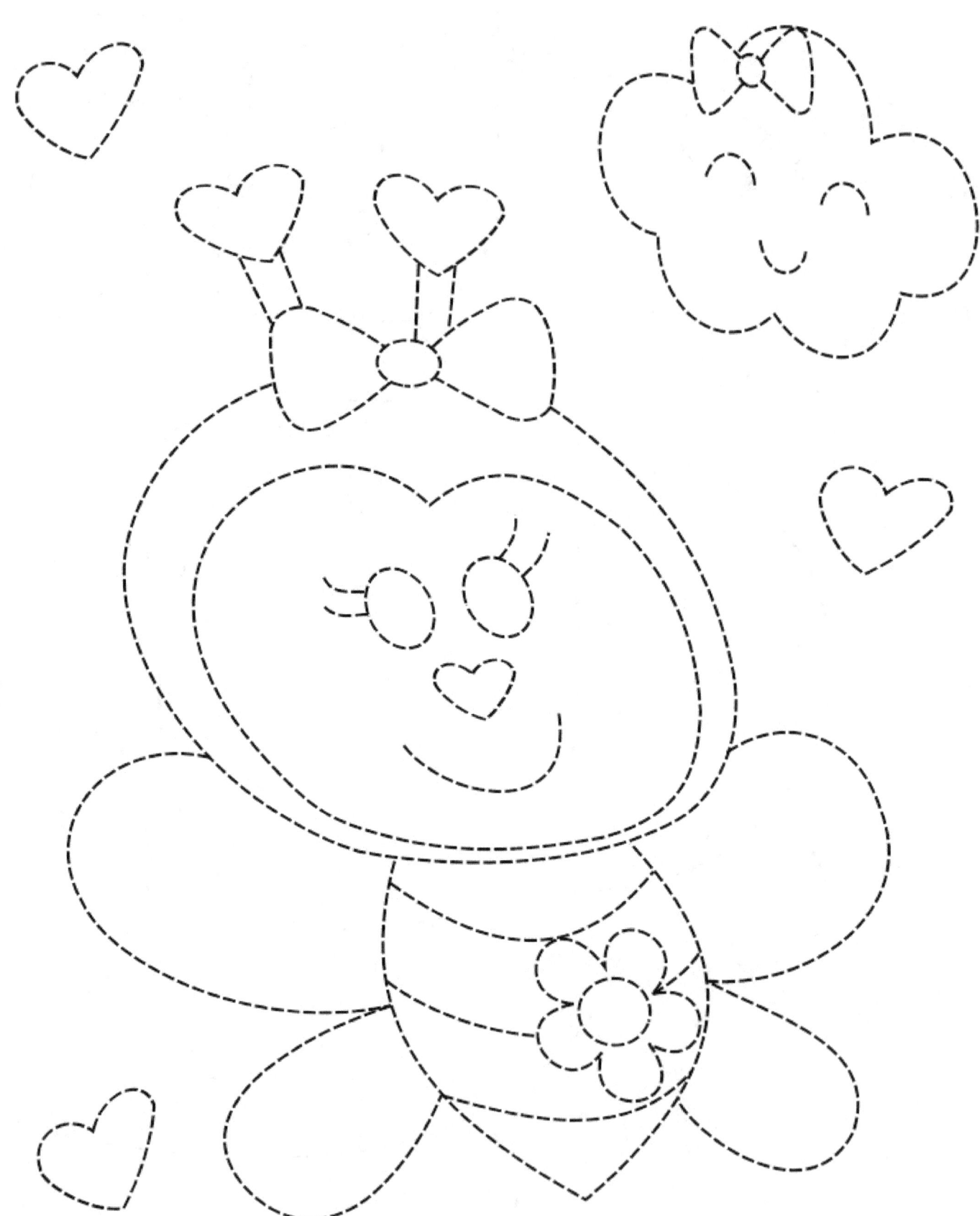

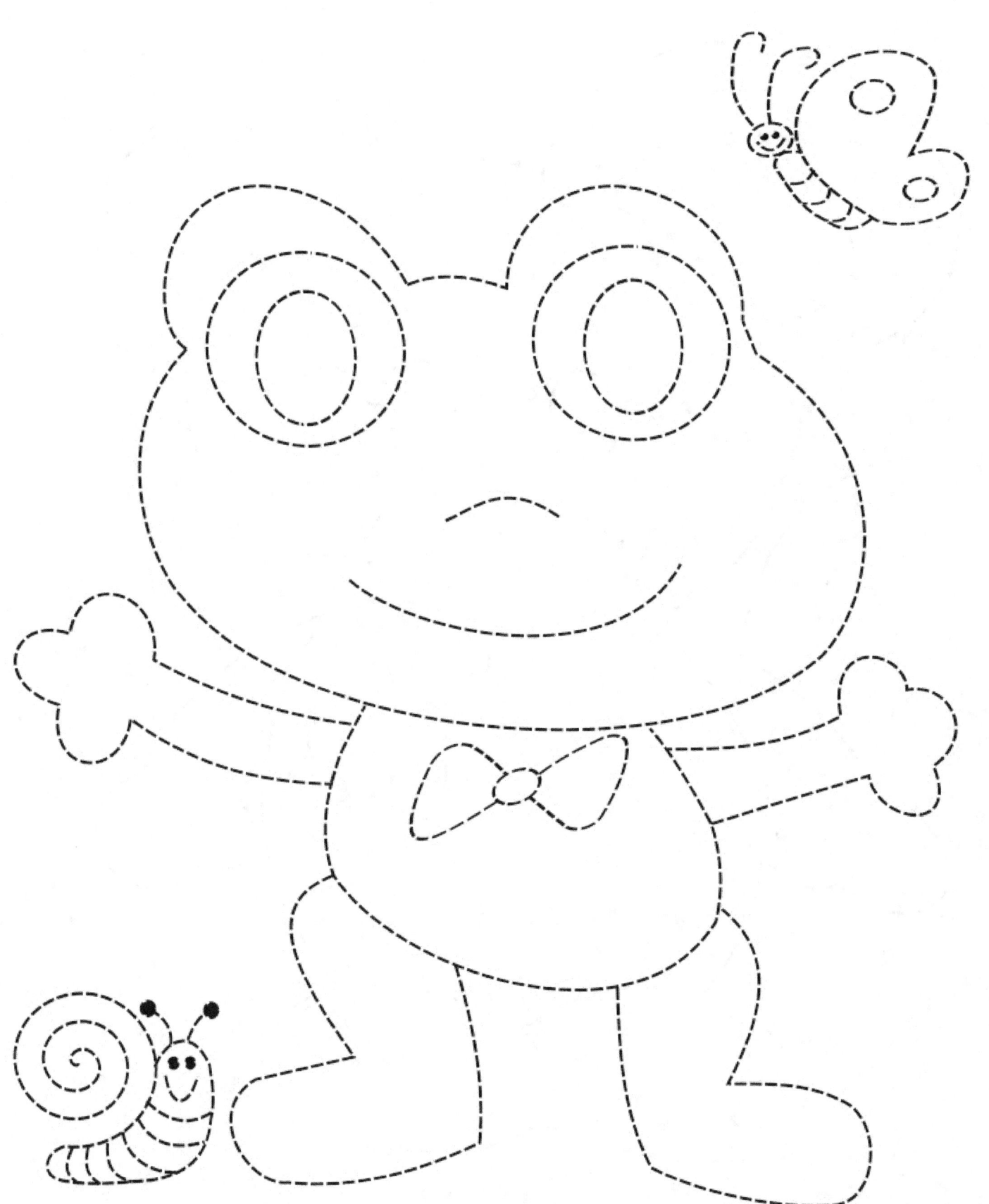

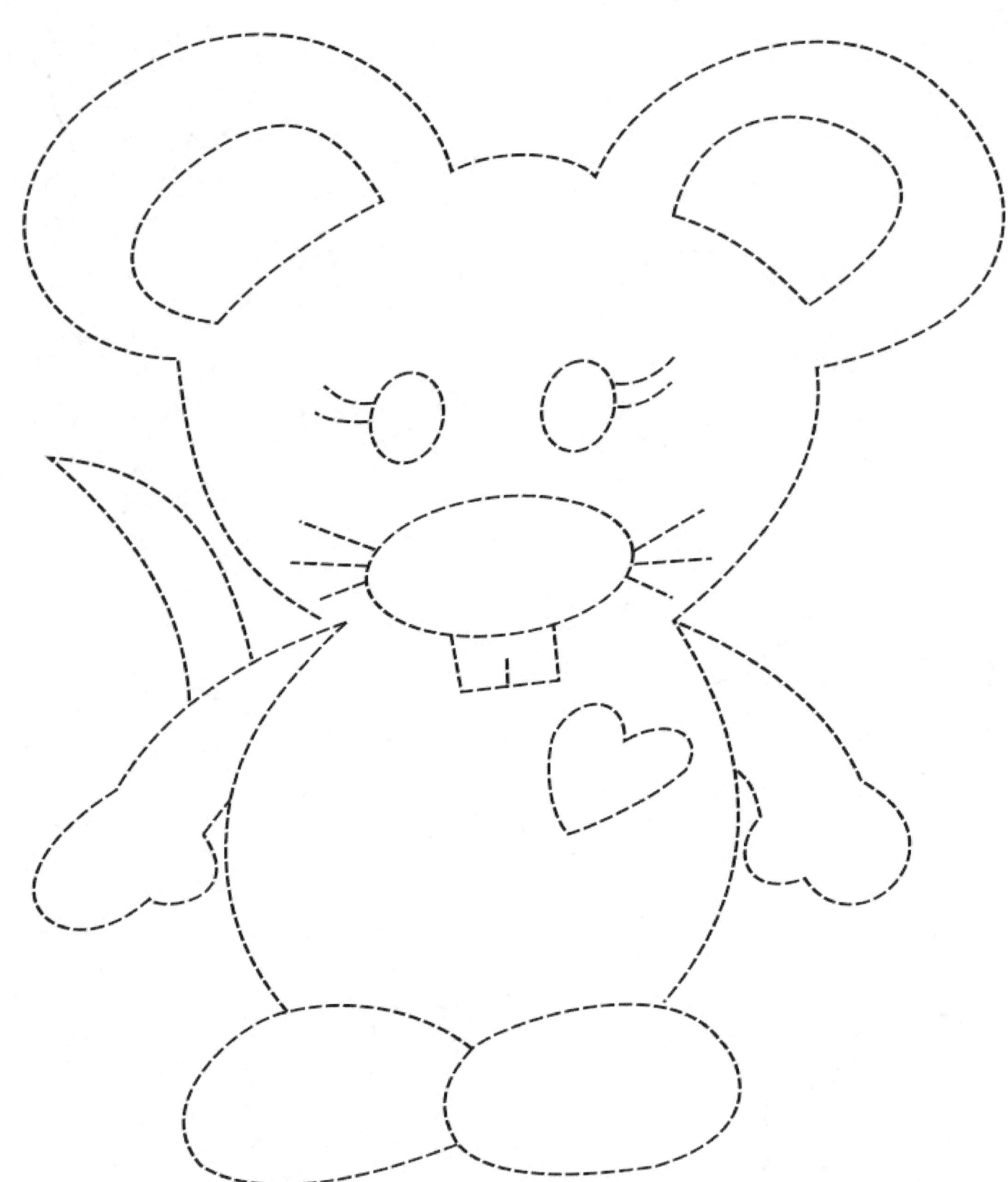

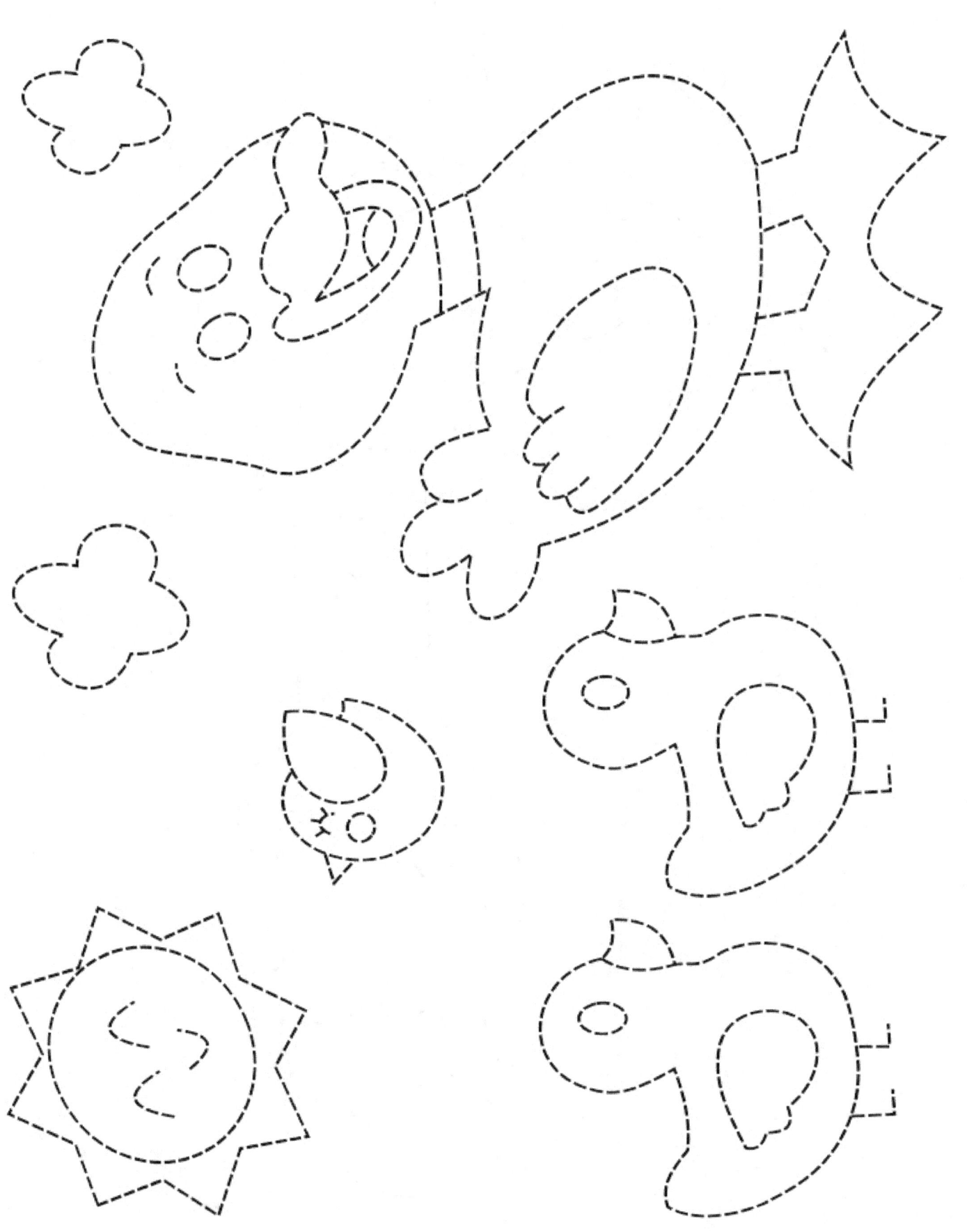

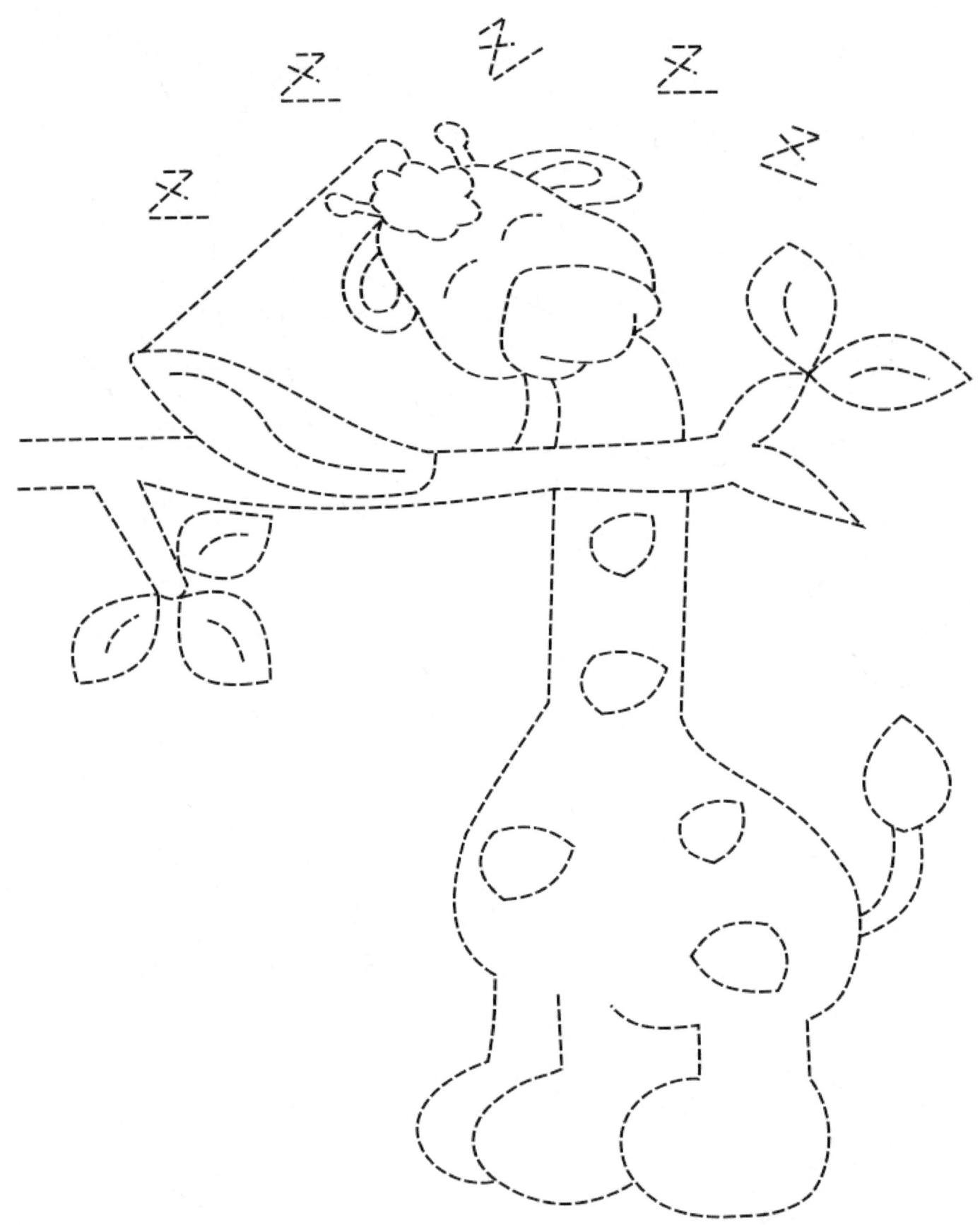

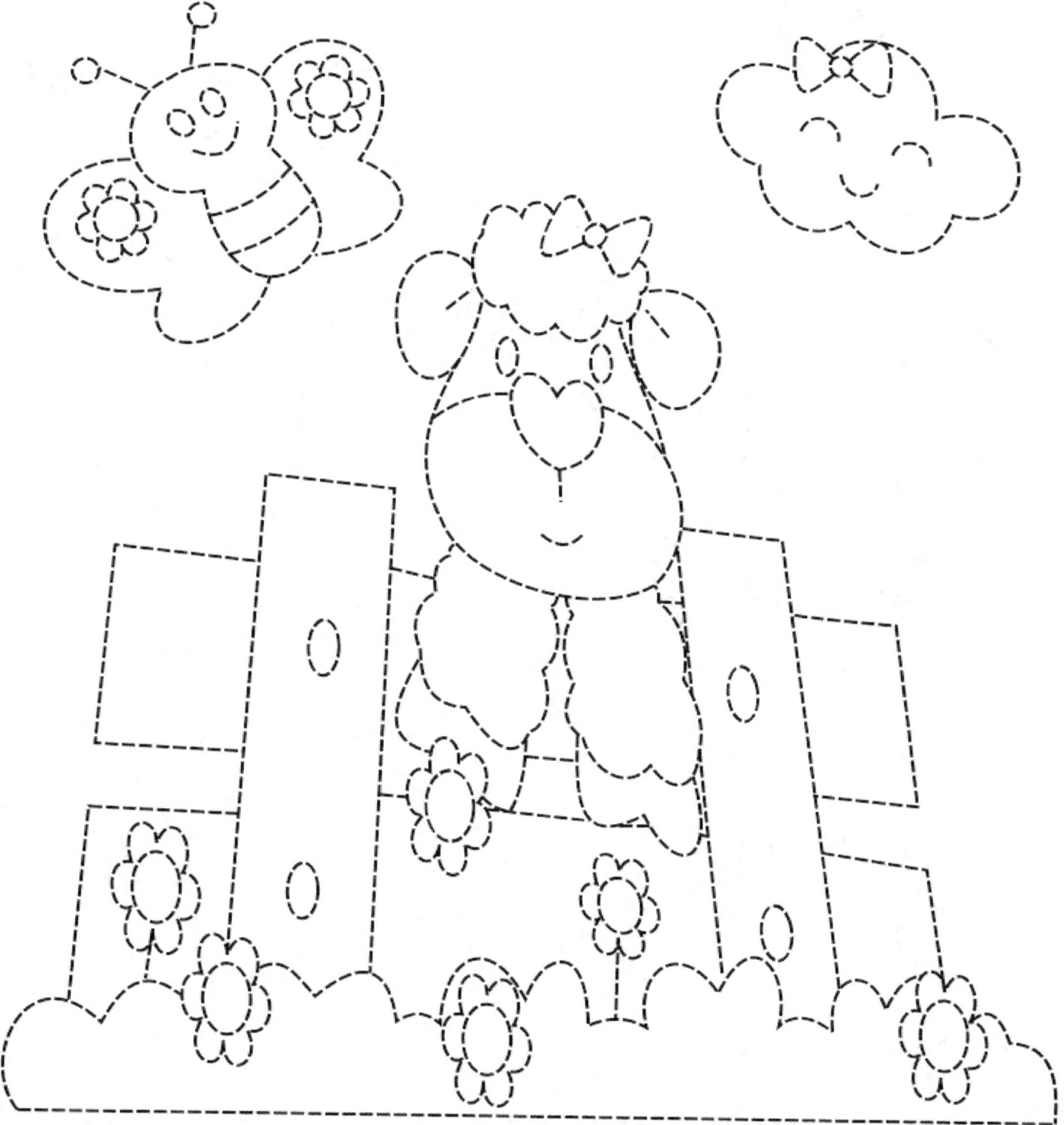

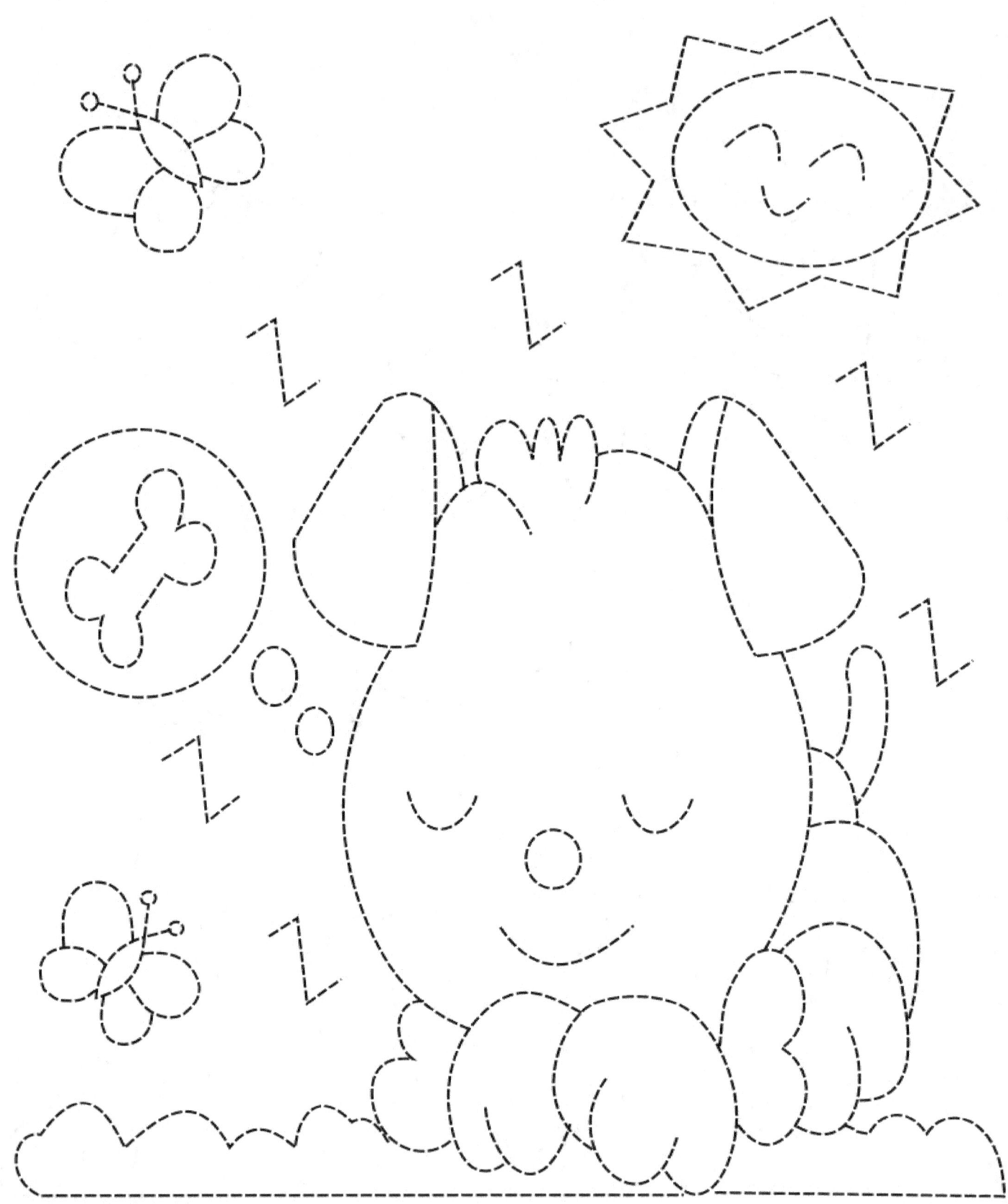

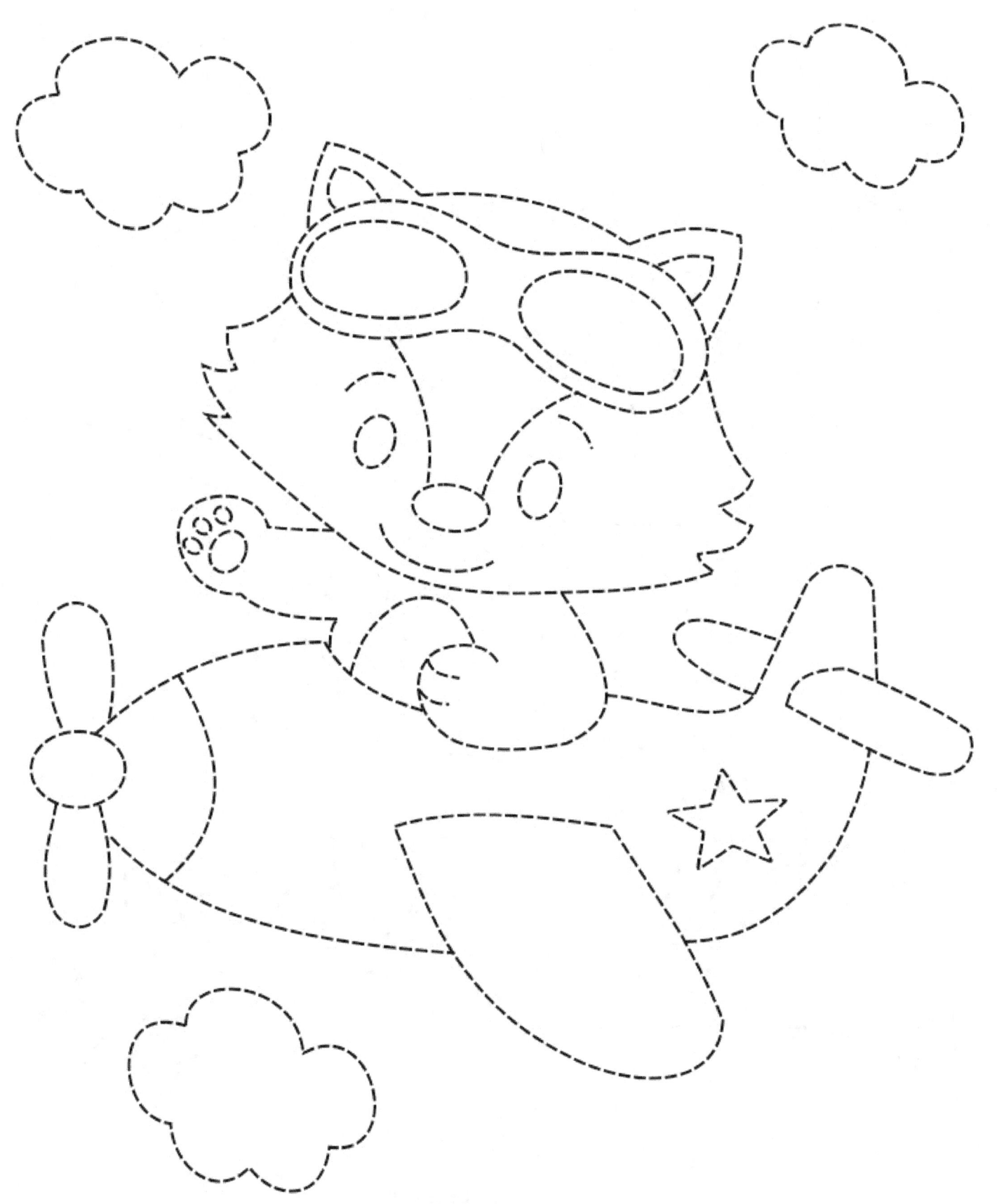

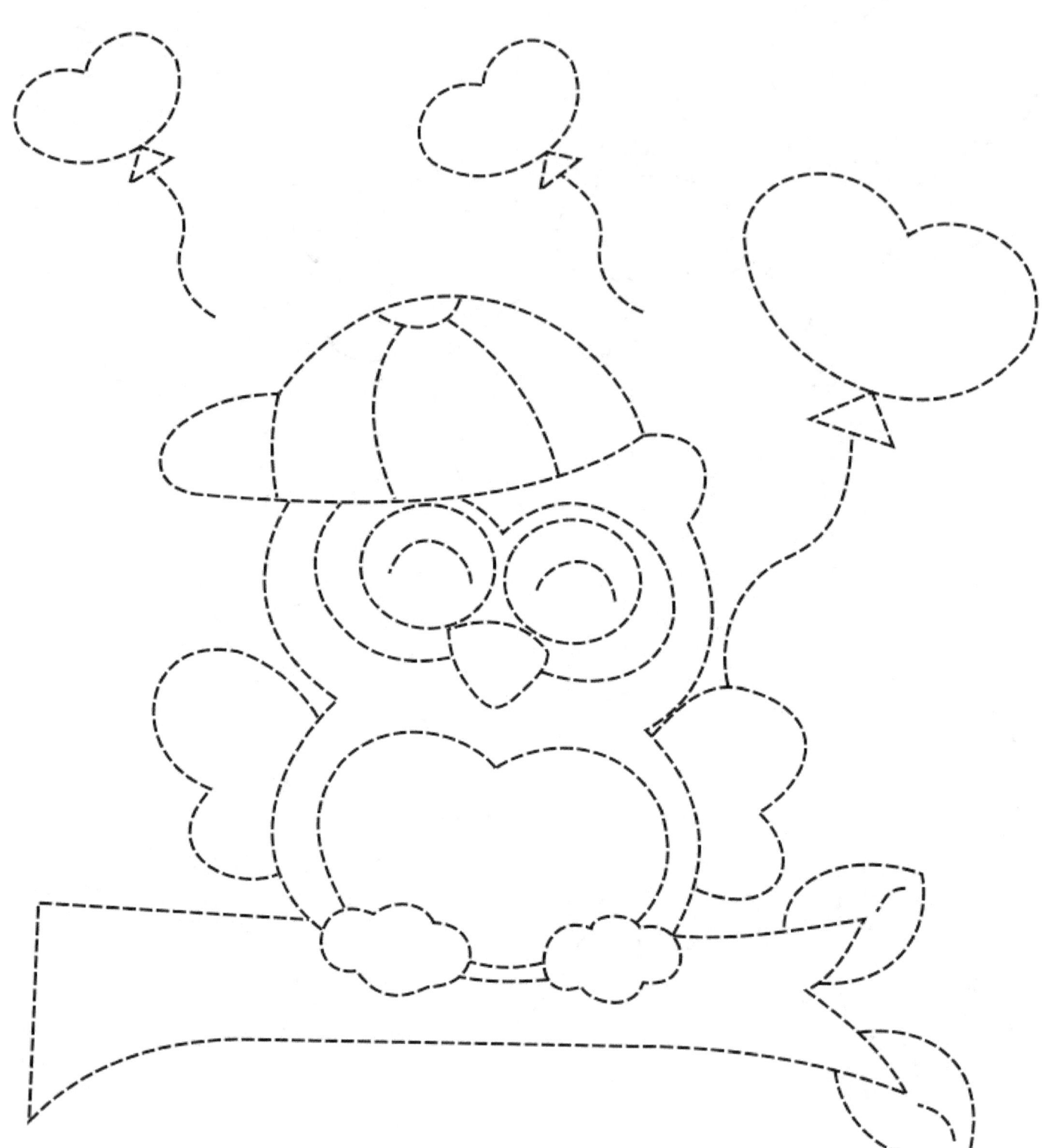

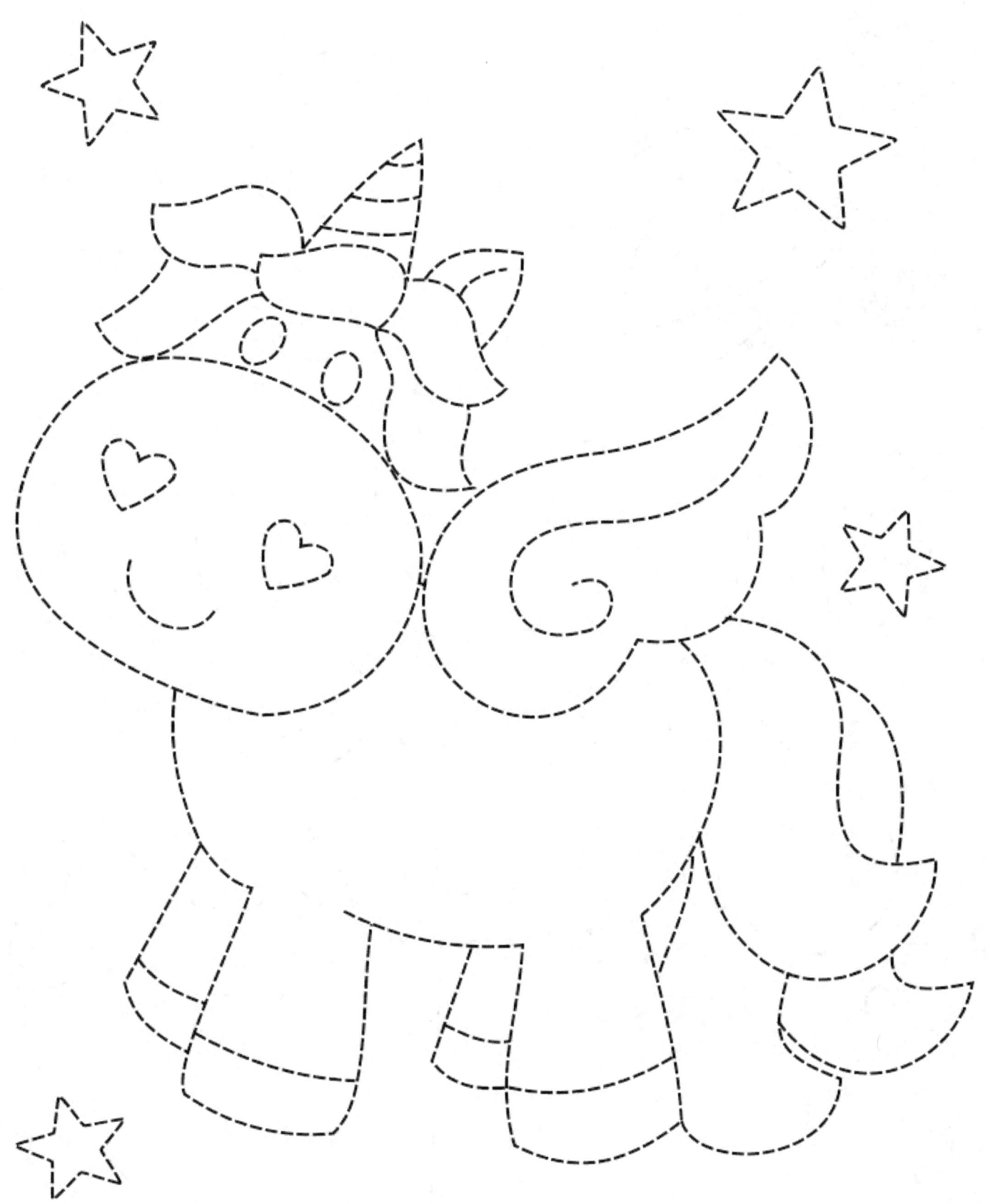

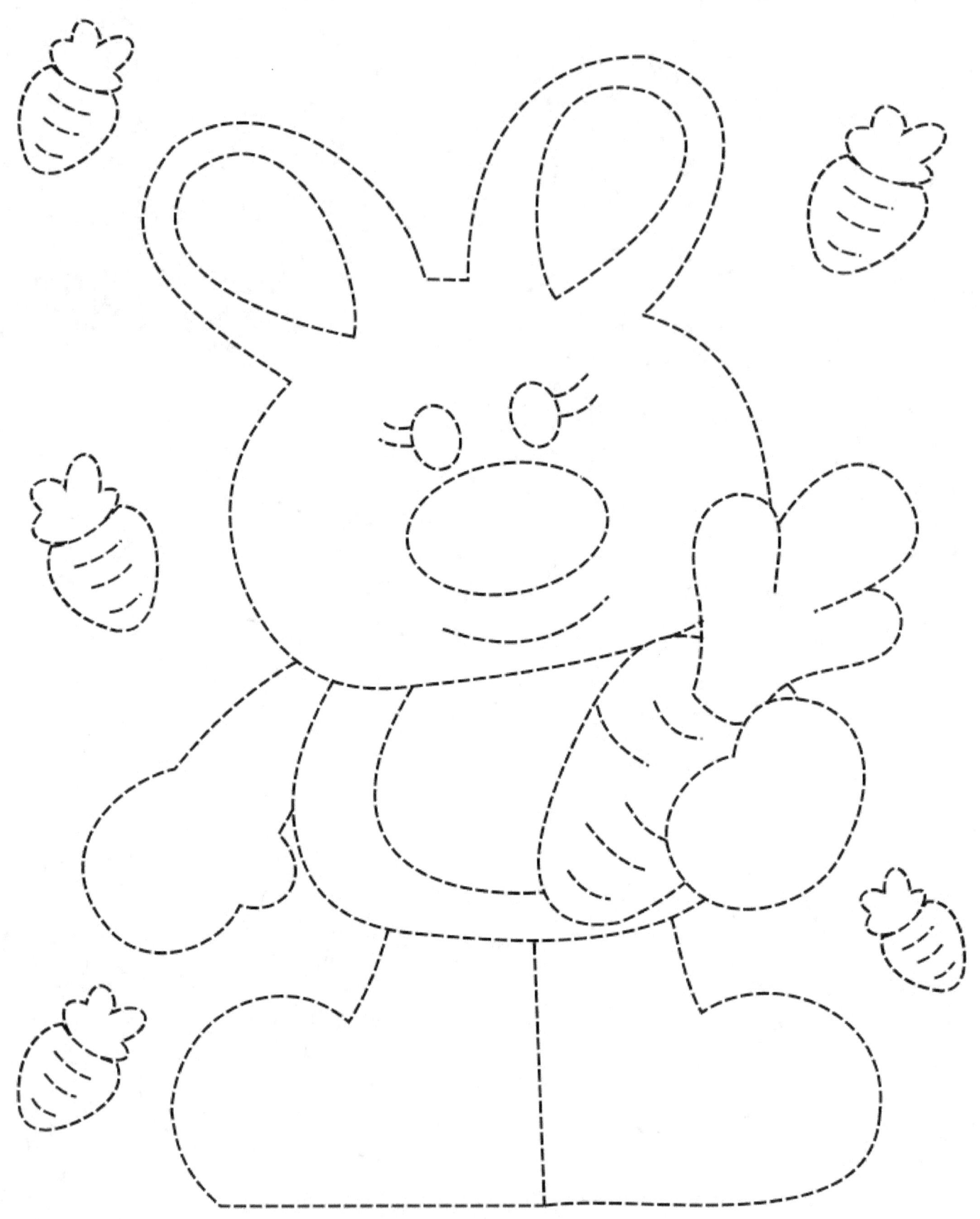

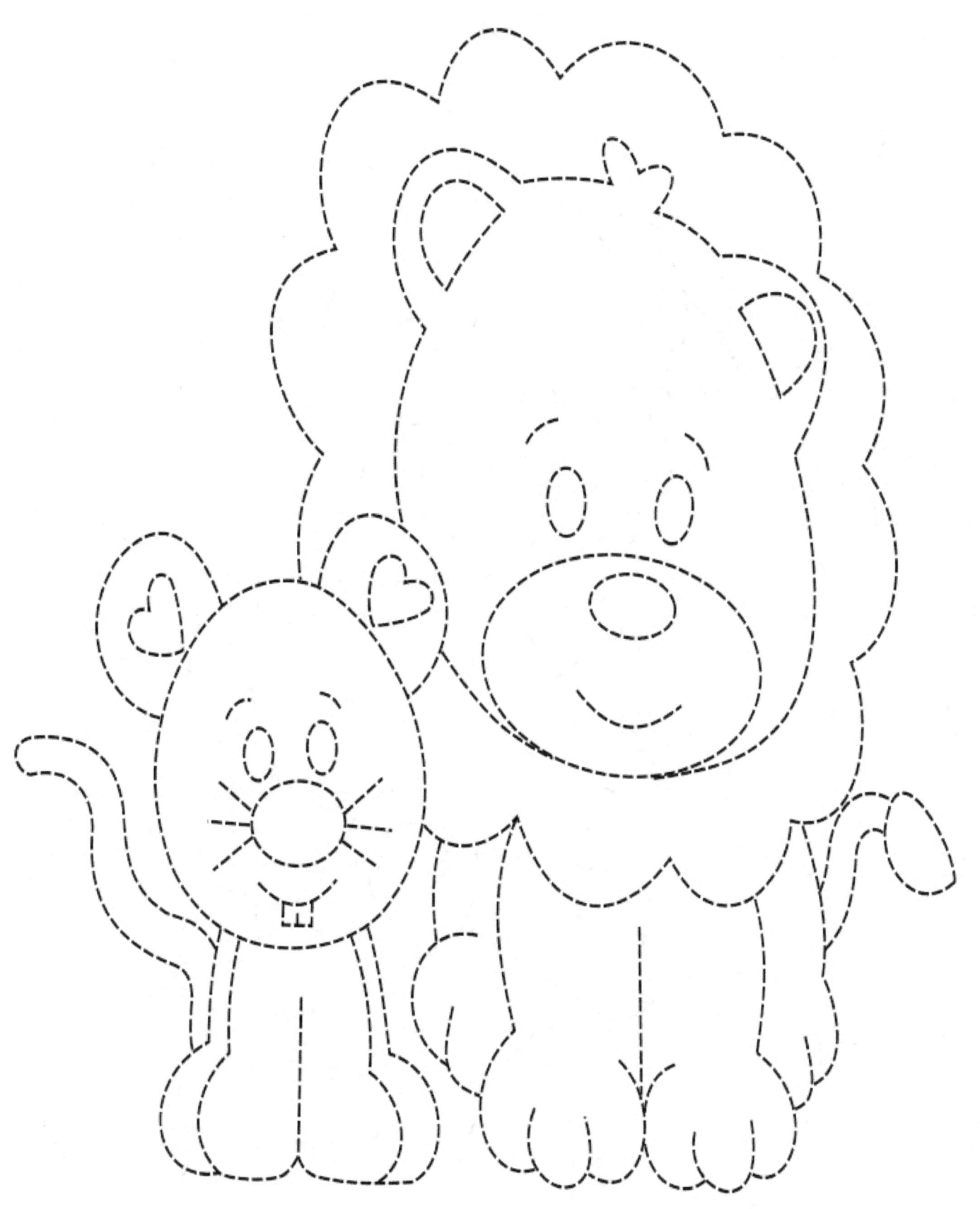

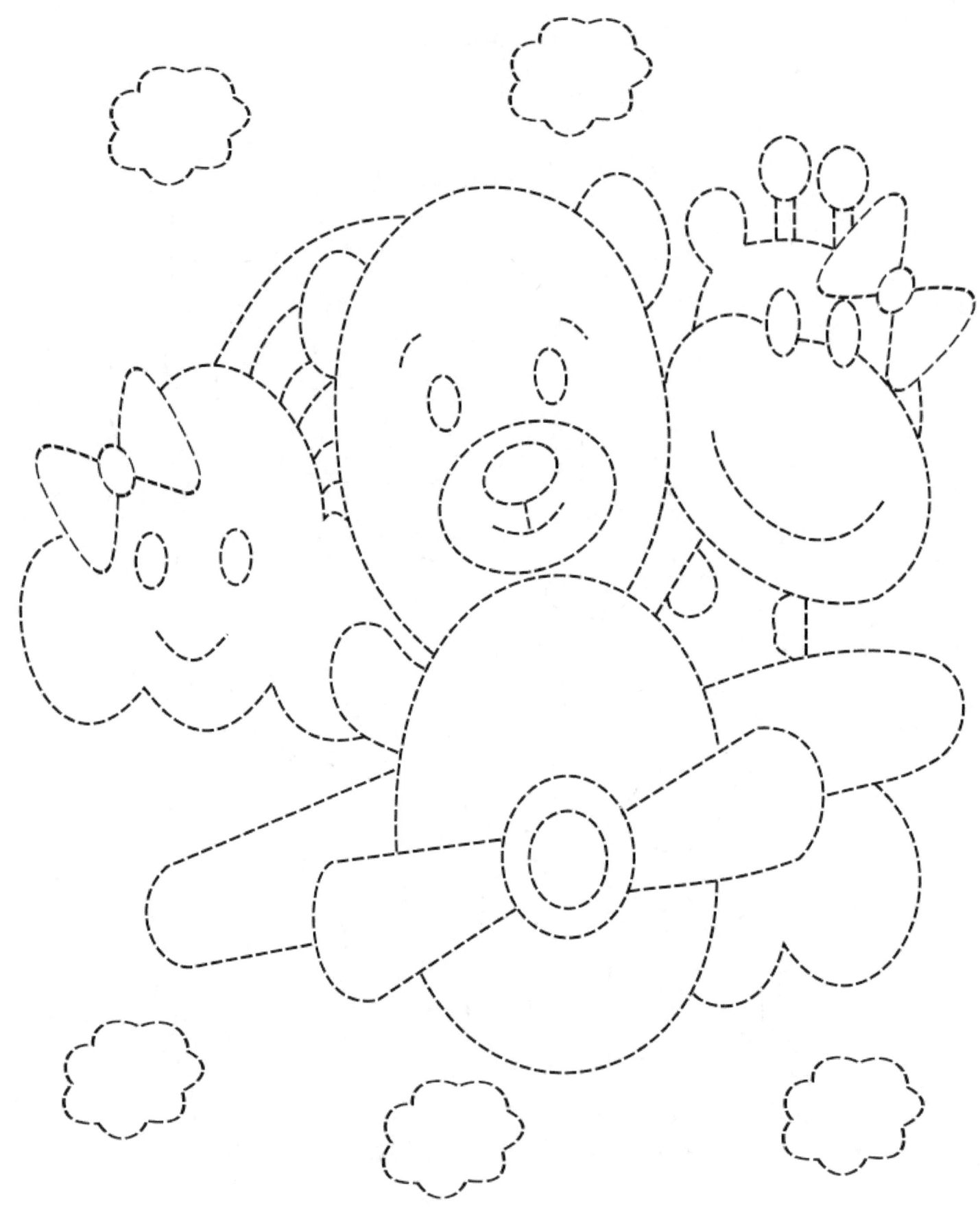

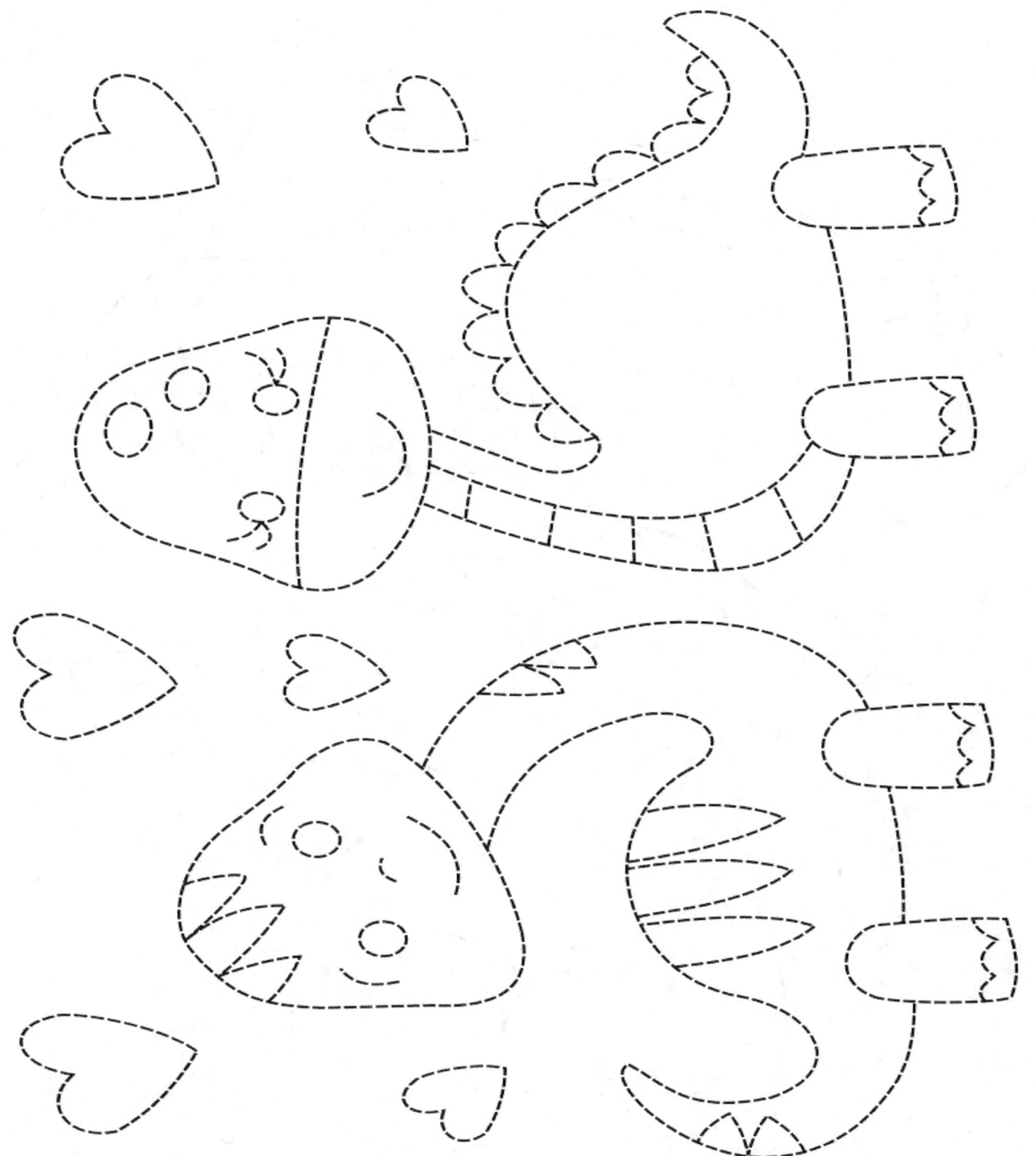

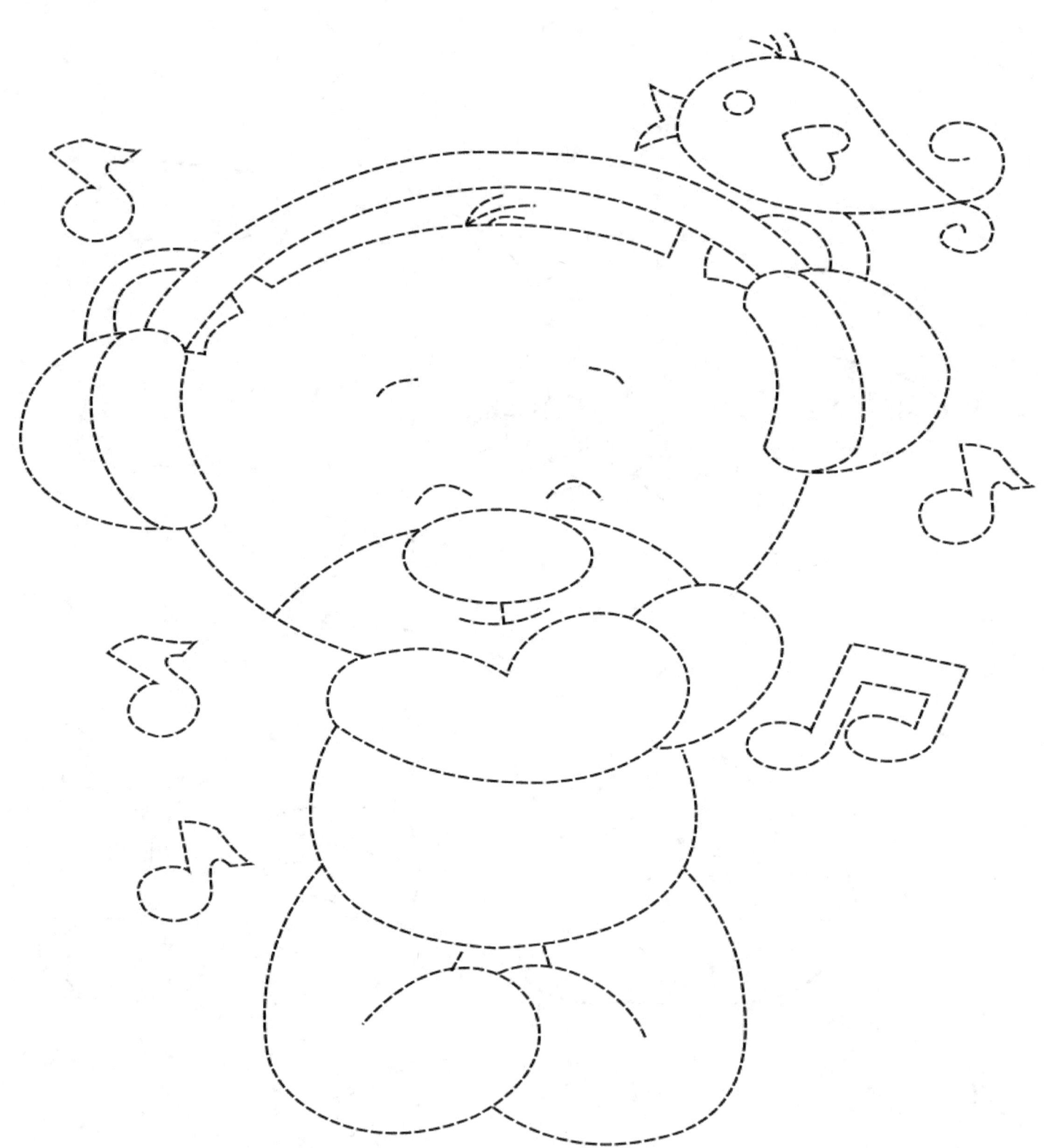

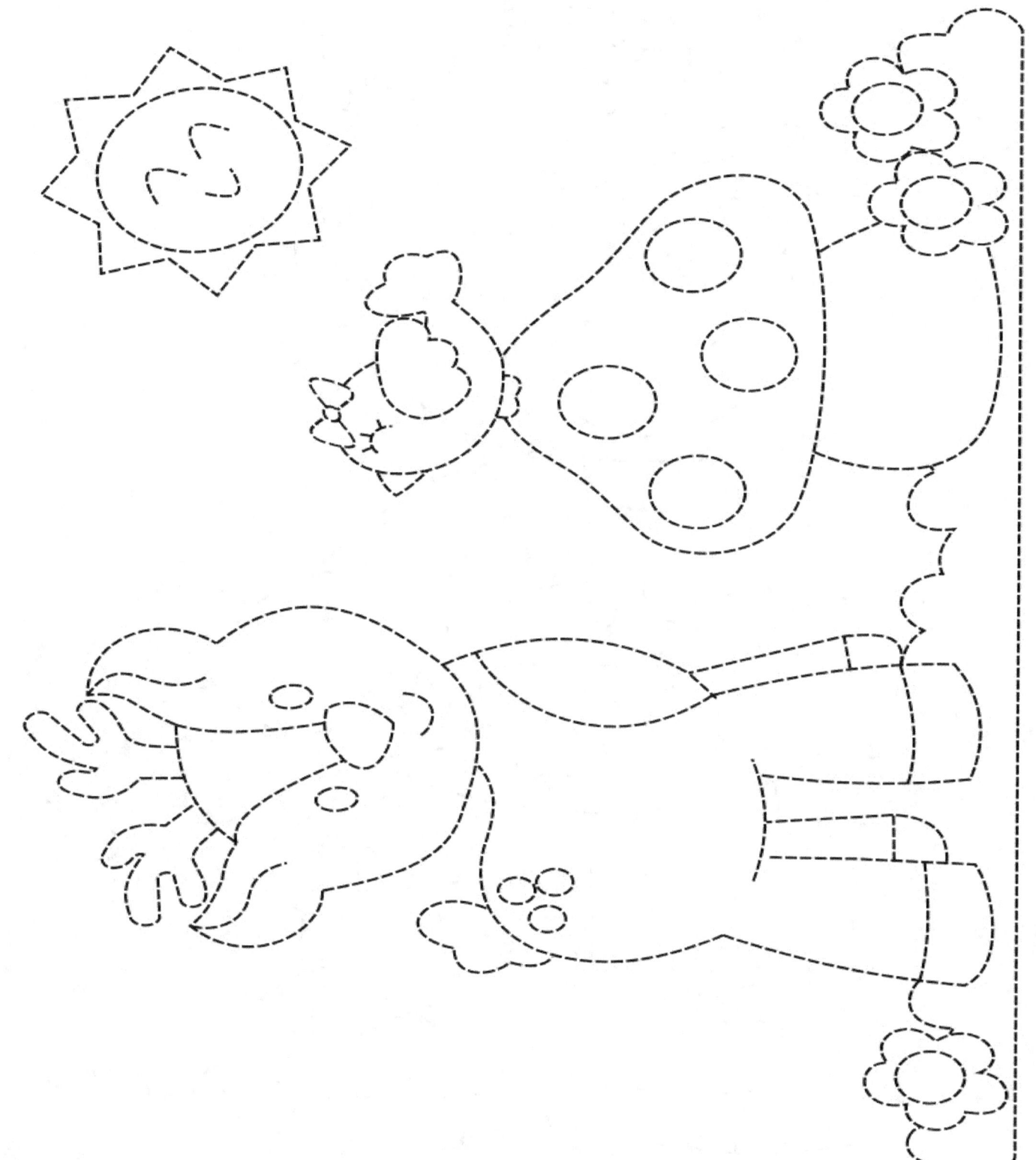

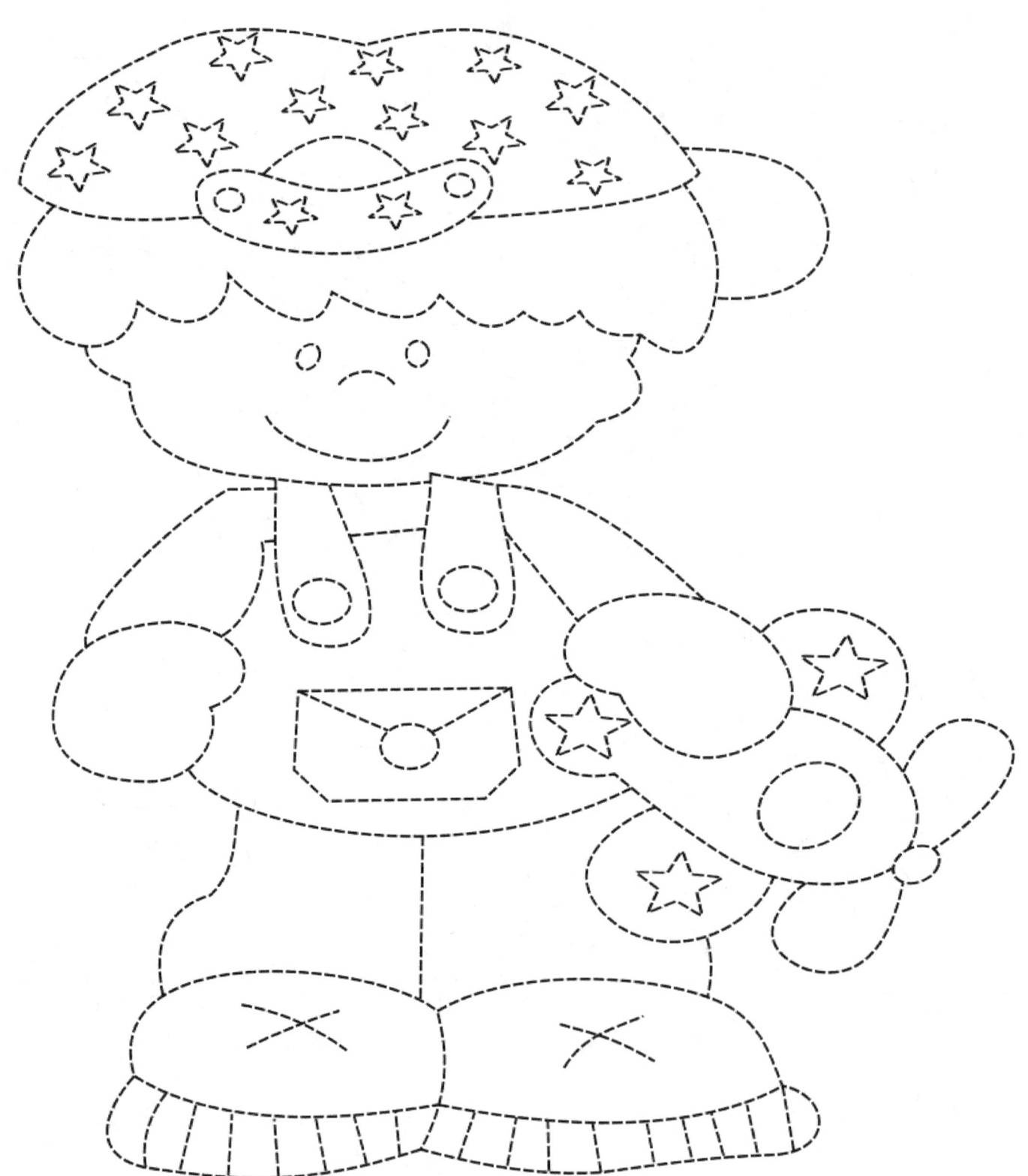

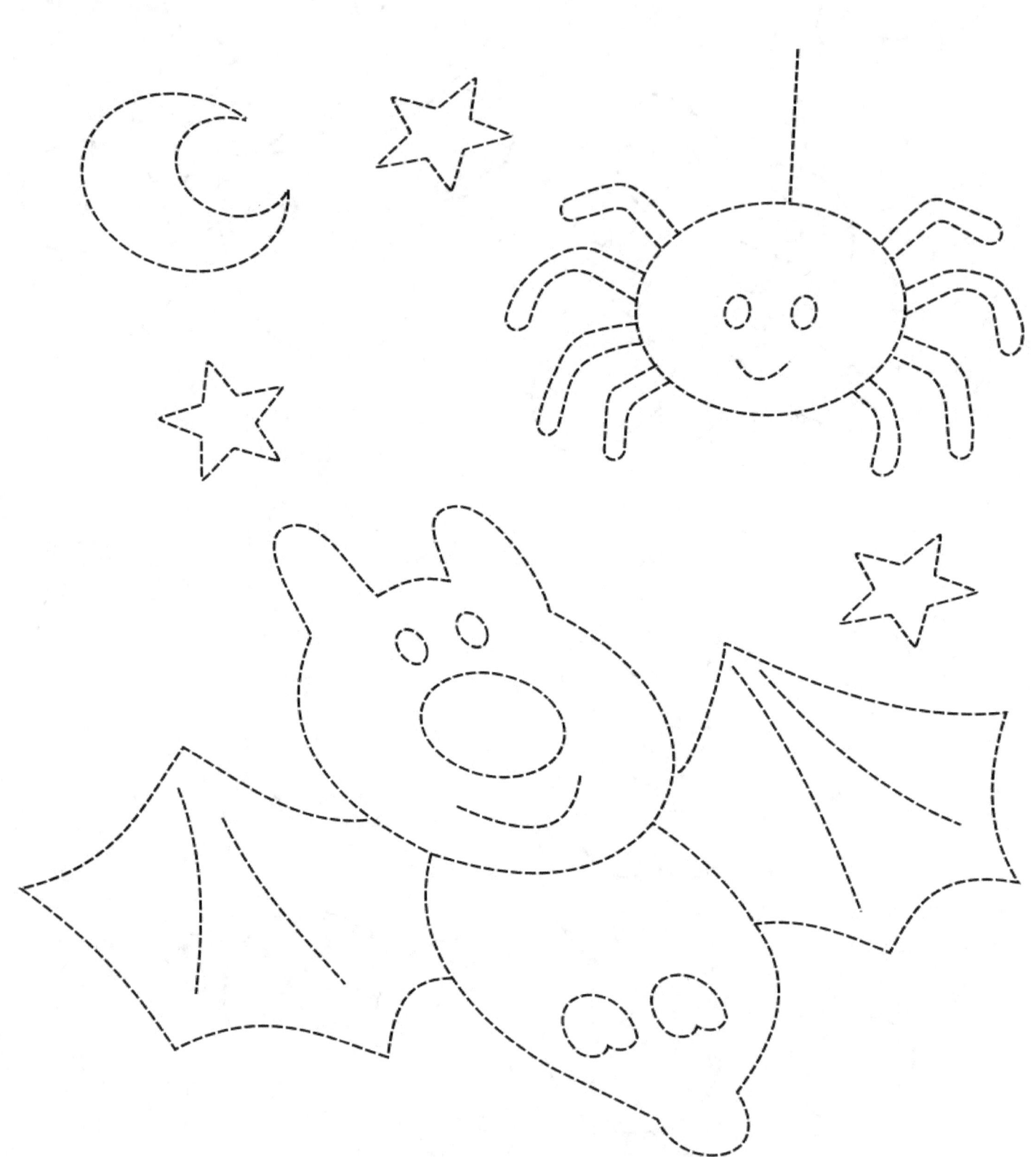

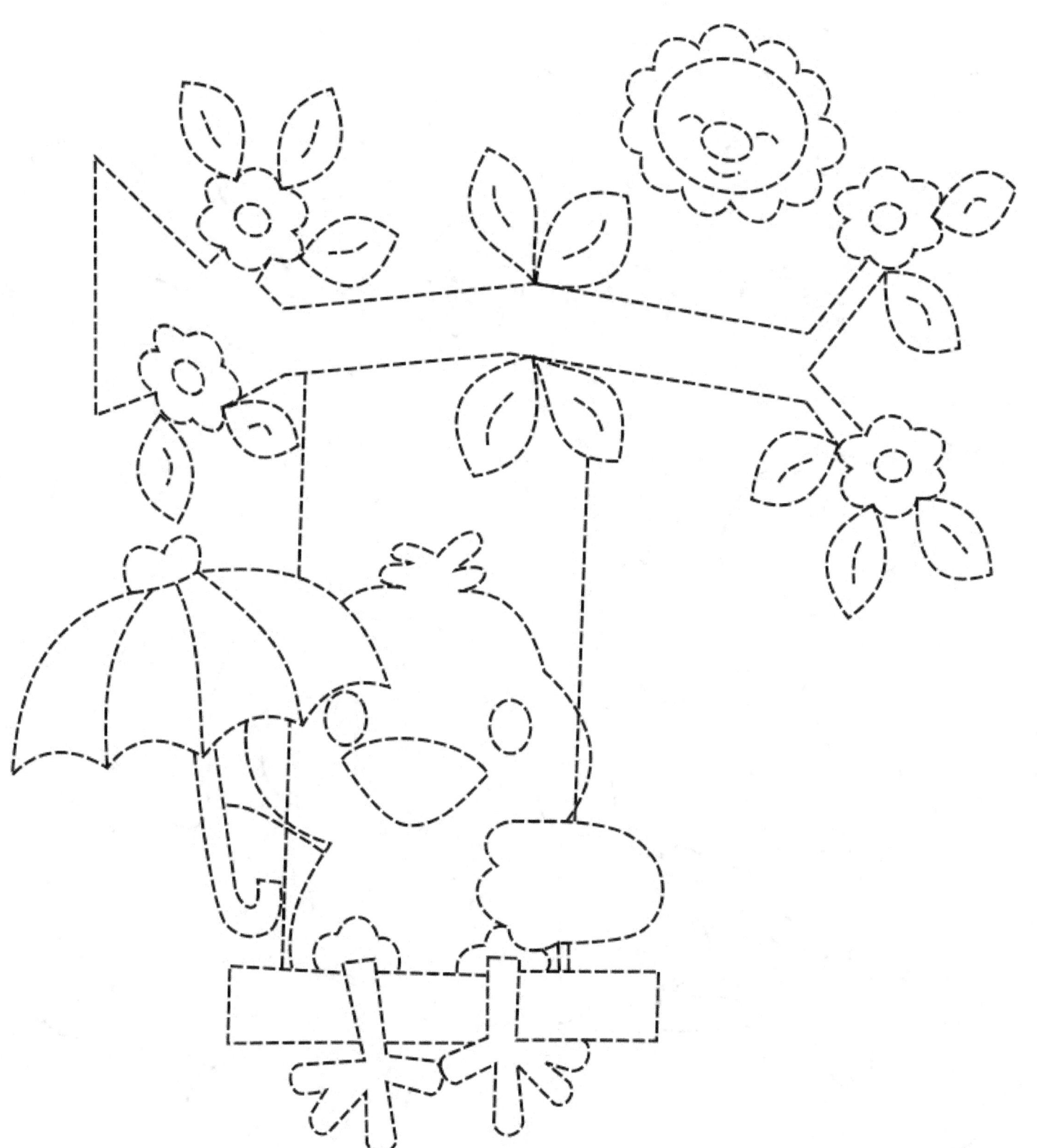

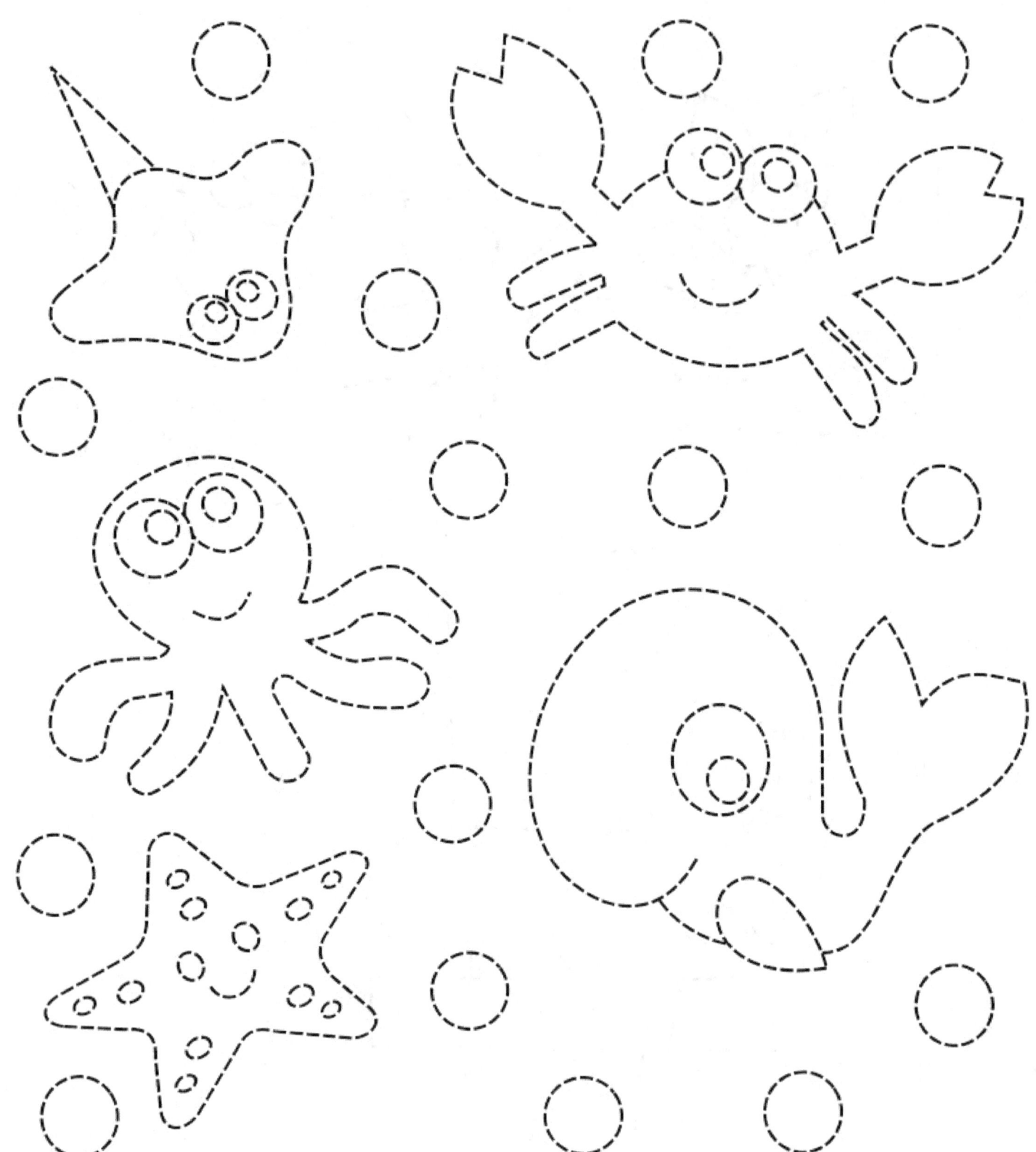

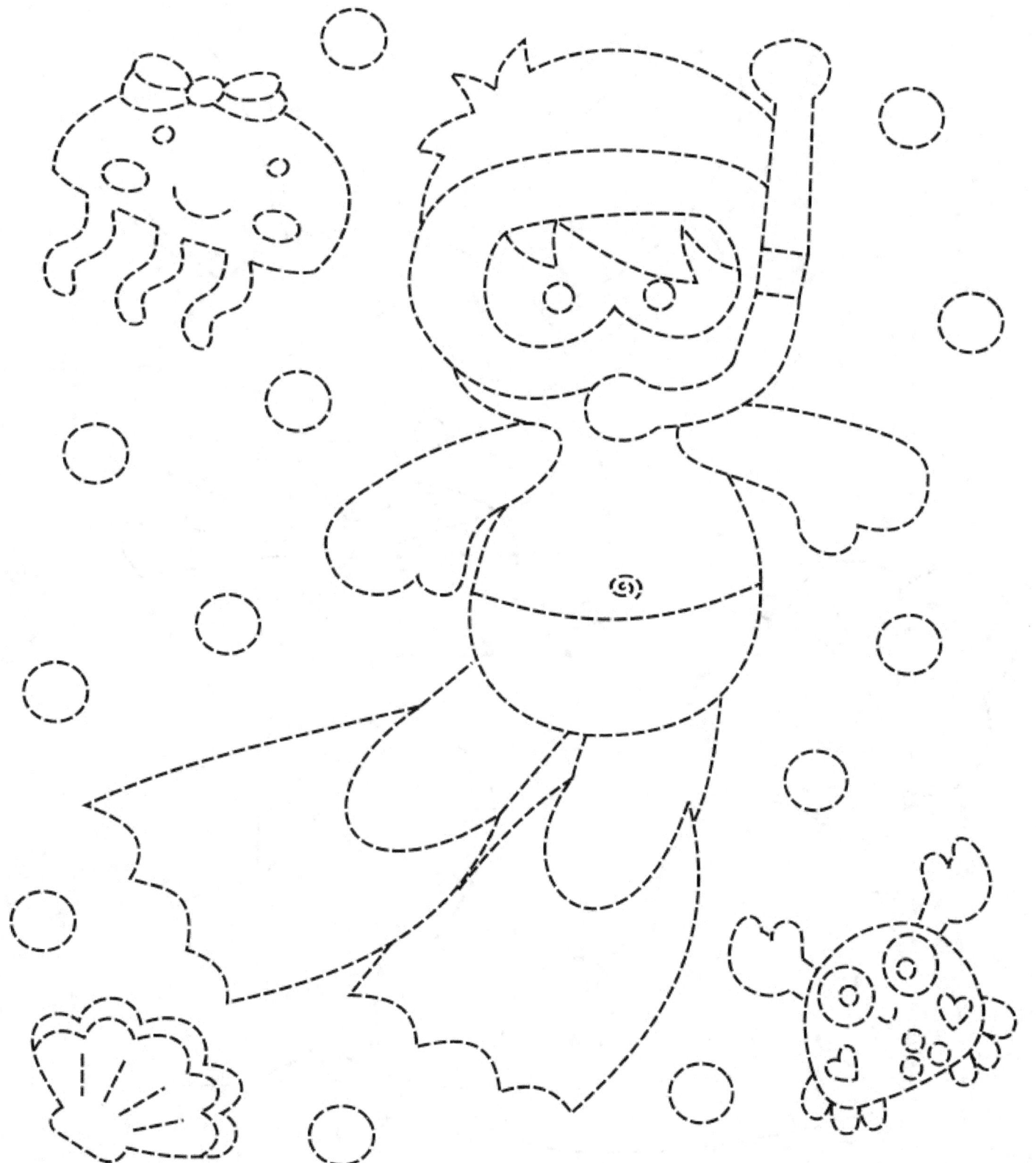

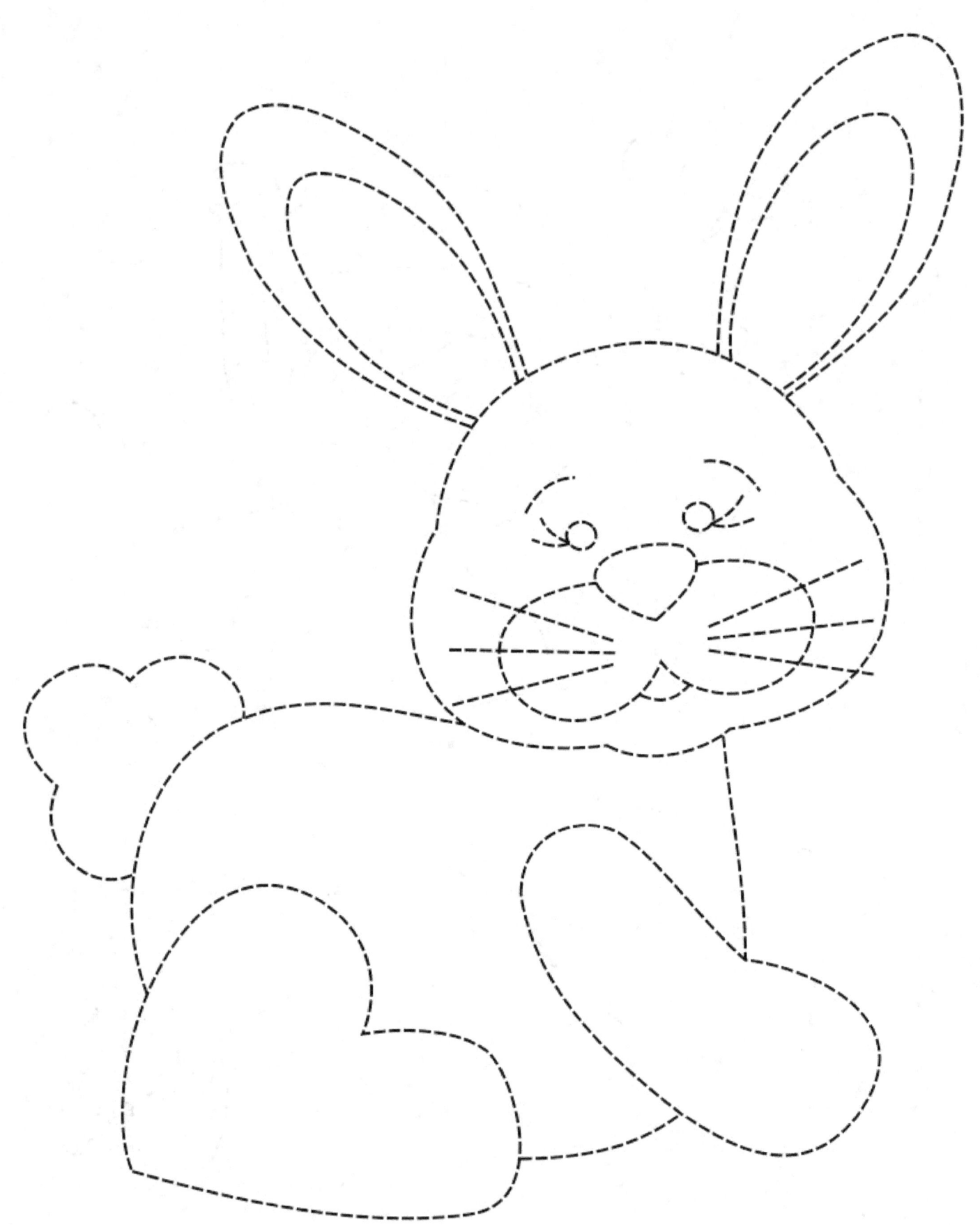

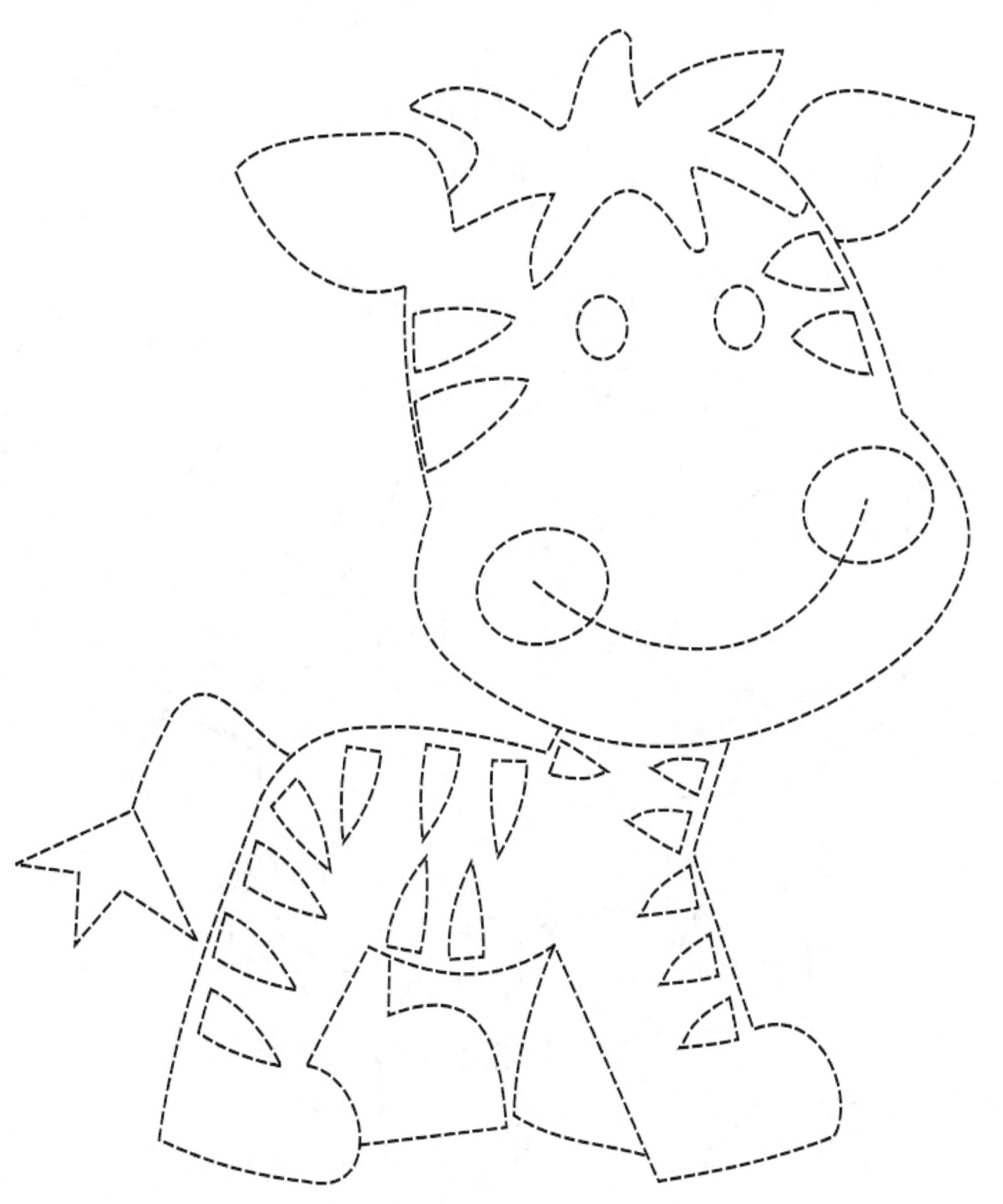

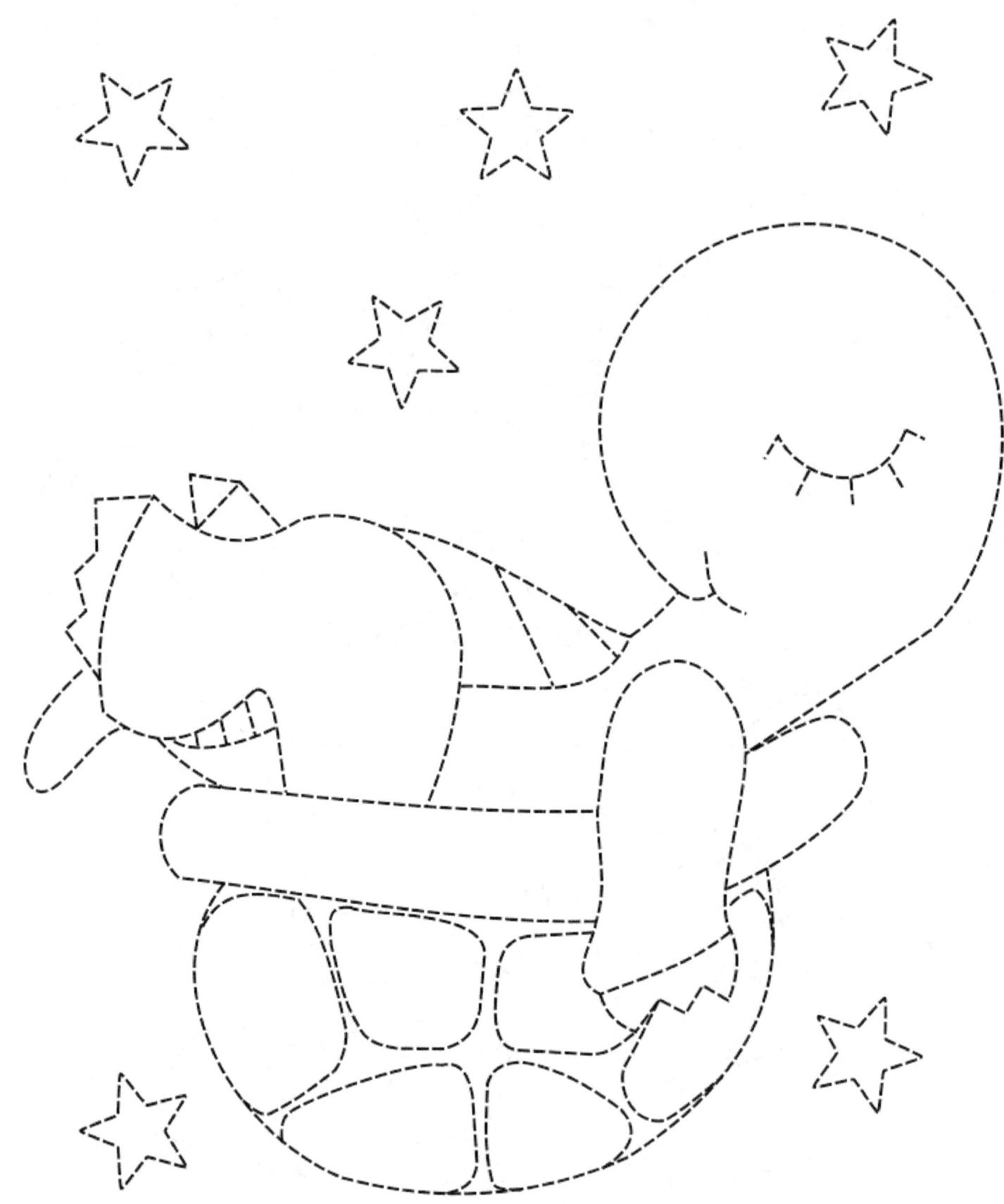

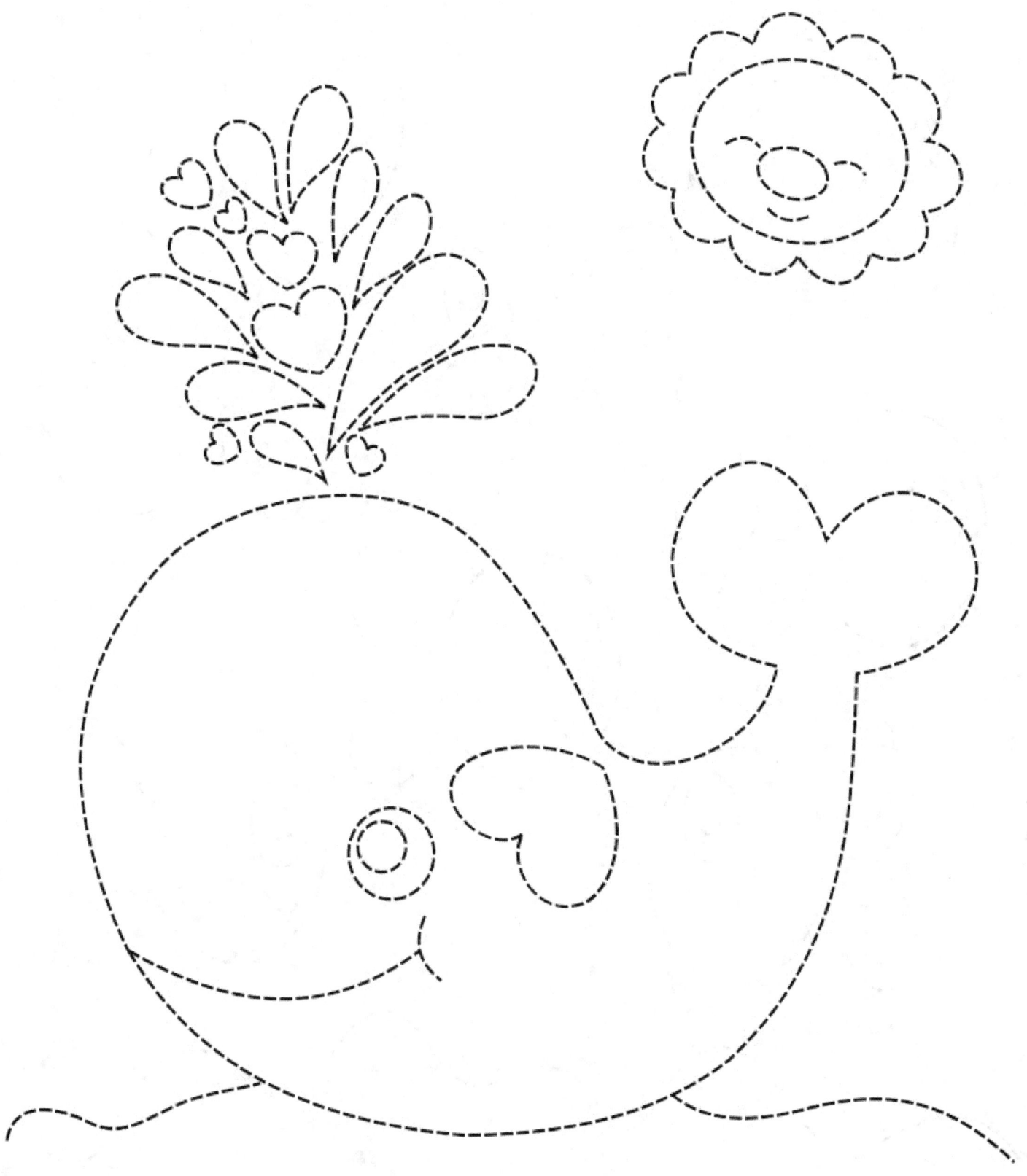

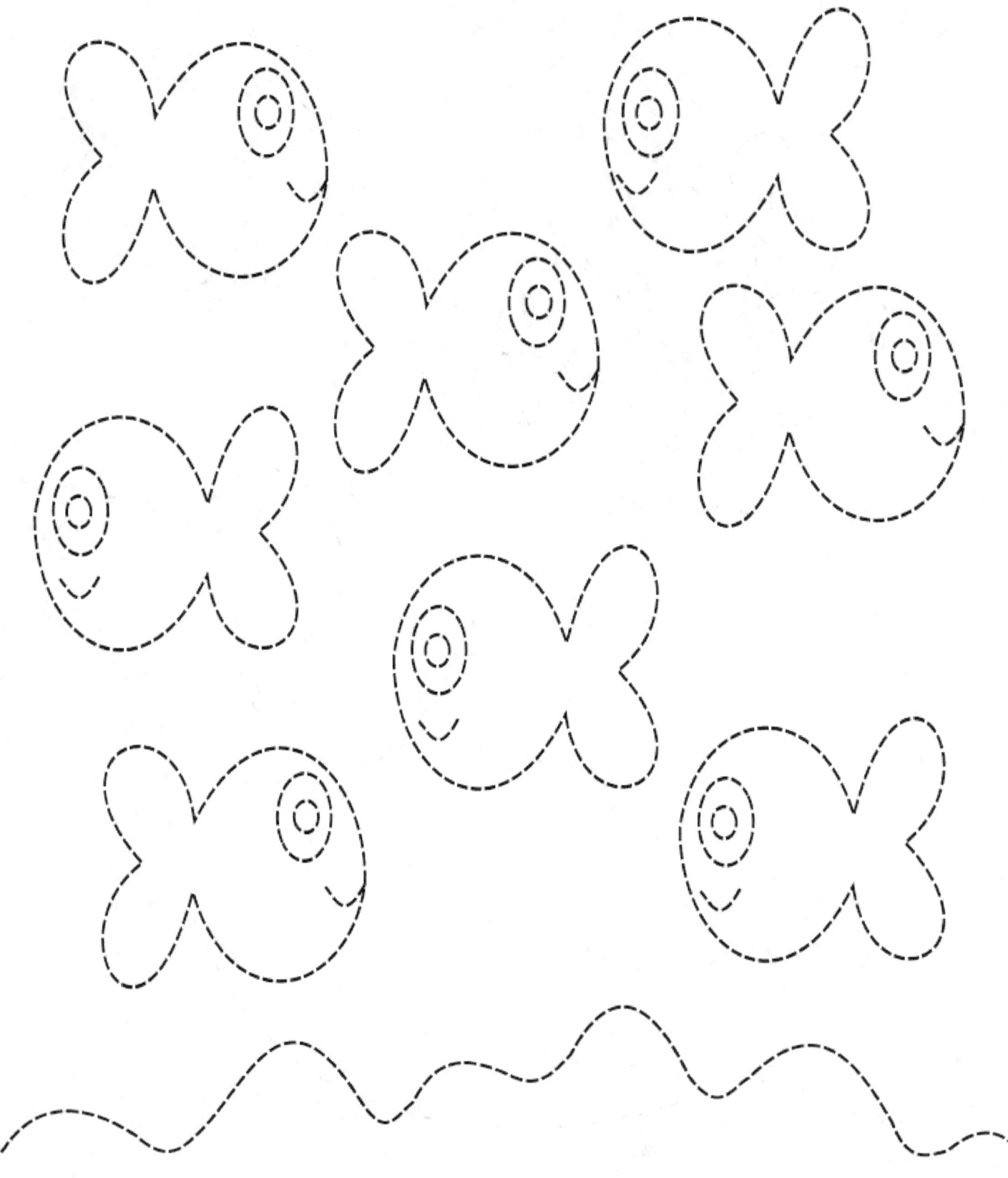

www.ingramcontent.com/pod-product-compliance
Lightning Source LLC
Chambersburg PA
CBHW080442220526

45465CB00007B/2737